INVISIBLE APPLIQUE

By Ami Simms

Illustrations by
Jean Pajot Smith

MALLERY PRESS
Flint, Michigan

DEDICATION

This book was written for anyone who has ever tried traditional applique, didn't like it, and thought it was their fault.

It is dedicated to my students, who always seem to ask the right questions at the right time, and to my family without whose help and support this book could not have been written. The former got the creative juices flowing and let me practice on them first, and the latter gave me guilt-free time to travel, teach, and write.

Special thanks to Lola Choinski, whose demonstration of the ladder stitch inspired me to give applique a try; to Casey Hill for allowing me to place each line of type *exactly* where I wanted it; and to Jean Smith, who can draw whatever is in my mind's eye.

Library of Congress Cataloging in Publication Data
Simms, Ami, 1954-
  Invisible Applique
1. Applique   I. Title.
TT779.S56   1988   746.9'7 88-1617
ISBN 0-943079-01-2

CONTENTS

INTRODUCTION

Invisible Applique is a "ladder stitch" that even beginners can master to create smooth curves, sharp points and precise placement of applique designs, all with a thread that barely shows.

Unlike traditional applique, sewing lines are marked on both the piece to be appliqued, and on the background fabric. Stitches are then taken alternately in each piece, with the needle moving along the sewing lines in a straight path, instead of at an angle. Seam allowances are turned under with the tip of the needle as the applique is sewn, keeping fabric preparation to a minimum. Best of all, it is a stitch that doesn't take years to perfect.

Invisible Applique is not only easy to learn, it is versatile as well. In almost a dozen years of quiltmaking I have found no other stitch which offers as many possibilities. It is the perfect stitch for any applique pattern, from Whig Rose to Clamshell, and can be used to create Stained Glass, Reverse Applique, Hawaiian, and Pictorial quilts too. It is a great way to sew down a binding, and the only way I've found to repair damaged or worn patches in finished pieces. You can even hand piece with it! Aside from the quilting stitch, this may be the only other stitch you'll ever need.

The book is divided into three sections. The first part gives step by step instructions designed to teach you the basic stitch. By working through each exercise you will learn to sew straight seams, corners, concave and convex curves, points, V-shapes, and circles. You can stop there, never read another word, and go off happily into the sunset creating beautiful applique.

Or, you can read the second part of the book, and explore some other uses for this wonderful stitch, some of which are outlined above. Who knows, you may have always wanted to make a Stained Glass Clamshell in Reverse Applique with little pictorial scenes inside each "shell." Now you'll know how.

If you're ready for adventure, move on to the third and final section of the book for a lesson in hand piecing using Invisible Applique. If you thought regular applique was fun, wait till you try this! When you're finished it will look exactly like traditional hand piecing, except that your points and corners will match better, and it will have taken less effort. And, you can show all your friends your obviously pieced looking quilt and tell them you APPLIQUED it. Then pick them up off the floor and show them how you did it!

PART ONE: MASTERING THE STITCH

Welcome to the world of applique! If you've tried traditional applique and found the results less than satisfying, you're in for a treat. With Invisible Applique, you can look forward to smooth curves, sharp points, and perfect placement of each applique design. Fabric preparation is kept to a minimum, sewing lines will help guide your needle, and the mechanics of the stitch are easily mastered.

The exercises below will teach you all you need to know about the stitch itself. In just a short time you will have the skill and confidence to tackle ANY applique project. And, best of all, you'll wonder how you got so good so fast.

CHAPTER I
PREPARATION

Fabric

While Invisible Applique can be used on any fabric, beginners should first try it on quilting weight, 100% cotton as it is the easiest to work with. Cotton does not ravel as quickly as some polyester blend fabrics, and is easier to control because it shifts and slides less.

Use only fabrics which have been washed, dried, tested for colorfastness, and pressed.

For the exercises in the first part of this book, you will only need a handful of cotton scraps, template material, marking devices, NON-coordinating thread, and basic sewing supplies.

Templates

Begin by cutting a 2 inch square from your template material. Mark the RIGHT side of the template so that each time the template is placed on the fabric the same side is facing up. On clear plastic template material I often hand-write something on the right side. If I can read what I wrote, the template is right-side-up. If my writing is backwards, then my template is up-side-down. While this procedure may not always be necessary, it is a good habit to get into.

For shapes that appear to be identical, no

matter which way they are turned (clockwise/
counterclockwise, not top for bottom) such as
squares, rectangles, some stars and triangles, it
is a good idea to add an ORIENTATION MARK of
some sort as well. A star (or other small mark)
on one side of a square, for example, will simply
help you tell that side from the other three.
Since templates must be placed on the fabric
precisely each time, this can be a great help.

Orientation Mark on the 2 inch square template.

Grainline

So that the color of the applique pieces reads
consistently, and so that the pieces of fabric
handle predictably when sewing, make sure the
grainline in the background and the grainline in
the pieces to be appliqued are consistent.

The grainline should run VERTICALLY in all pieces both for sounder construction and for better appearance. The shapes of individual pieces to be appliqued do NOT determine grainline, and therefore may be placed anywhere on the field to carry out any design concept.

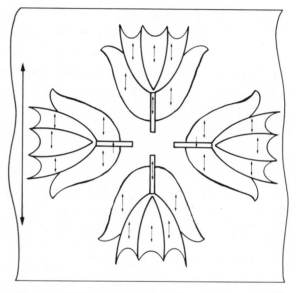

Keep grainline consistent and running vertically.

There are times, however, when grainline should be ignored altogether. When working with regularly patterned fabrics that are printed off grain, when sewing fabrics with directional designs, or when using prints that the artist wishes to incorporate into the design scheme in a way inconsistent with a vertical grainline, then the pattern on the cloth takes precedence over all grainline considerations.

Marking

Find the grainline of both the background
fabric and the piece of fabric to be appliqued.
Place the two pieces of cloth RIGHT side up, side
by side, with grainlines running vertically. Set
the 2 inch square anywhere, and at any angle
you prefer, on the background fabric. Since this
is merely a sewing exercise and no time whatever should be wasted fussing over which way
looks best, artistically place the template on the
fabric by closing your eyes and flinging it. As
long as all of it lands on the fabric and you have
a little around the outside edges to hang on to,
you're all set.

Trace around the template, and move it to
the fabric to be appliqued, *making sure that the
angle is the same.* Trace around again. All markings should be on the RIGHT side of the cloth.

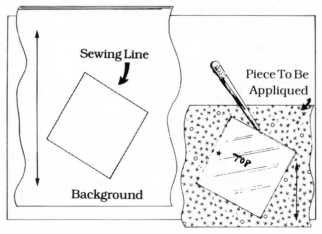

Carefully mark each piece on the RIGHT side.

Be sure to use a marking device that gives you a clear, sharp line. It should wash out COMPLETELY. Bear in mind that there are times when even the most talented among us will mess up and our pieces may be a little off, exposing sewing lines that were supposed to be hidden. By marking with a substance that is completely removable, no one else need ever know.

If you mark in pencil or chalk, keep the point consistently sharpened, and remember to hold the marking tool at the same angle each time you trace around the template.

Lines should be thin, and as accurate as possible. Accidental double lines, stray marks, and sketchy lines will be confusing. Make sure corners are fully drawn and sharp, not rounded.

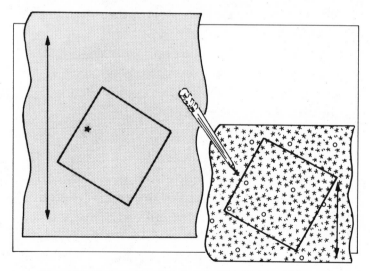

Transfer Orientation Mark to both pieces of fabric.

Transfer the Orientation Mark to both pieces. Put it in the inside of the square on the background piece and in the seam allowance on the piece to be appliqued, so that the marks will be hidden after the pieces have been sewn.

Cutting

The line made by tracing around the template is the sewing line. Trim around the sewing line on the piece to be appliqued so that 1/4 inch seam allowance remains. It is best to cut counterclockwise around the square when using right-handed scissors, with the discarded fabric falling to the right of the scissors, keeping the cutting line visible at all times.

To cut down on fraying, trim seam allowances just before you are ready to sew. Do not clip corners, and DO NOT fold, press, or baste the seam allowance under. For very small shapes, a seam allowance narrower than 1/4 inch may be used, but be sure there is still something left to turn under. Do not trim seam allowances narrower than 1/8 inch.

The Stitch

The Invisible Applique stitch is worked from right to left by right-handed quilters, and from left to right by left-handed quilters. The instructions and diagrams which follow are for right-handed quilters. Left-handed quilters are invited to turn to the Appendix.

CHAPTER II
LET'S GET TO IT

Getting Ready

It is essential that the stitch is begun at an easily recognizable point on both the piece to be appliqued and on the background. On a square, this would be any one of the four corners. If you start, instead, at a point along one of the sides, there would be no guarantee that you could find that same point on the other piece of fabric. Chances are great that you wouldn't come out even by the time you reached the first corner.

The stitch is worked in the twelve o'clock position. That is, were you to impose the face of a clock on your work surface, all the action would be going on at the TOP, or at the twelve. Since you will be sewing from right to left, (other way 'round for you lefties), start at the upper right-hand corner, (upper left-hand corner).

Lay the two pieces of fabric out in front of you, right sides up, so that the piece to be appliqued is on top of the background, with the Orientation Marks aligned. Slide the piece to be appliqued down just slightly to expose the sewing line of the background fabric. Turn your work so that you will be sewing along the top edge at all times.

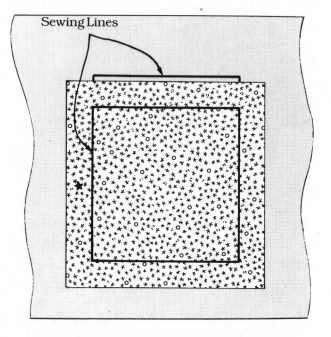

Both sewing lines are exposed.

Making The Stitch

When practicing, it is best to use contrasting thread so that any mistakes will be more easily seen, and hopefully corrected. Once you have mastered the technique, thread that matches the piece to be appliqued is preferable.

Thread your needle with a single thread about 12 inches long. Use regular hand sewing thread. A cotton wrapped polyester thread will be sturdy yet resist twisting and knotting. To cut down on fraying, you may wish to wax your thread before beginning.

Use a needle you are comfortable with. I use the same needle I quilt with as I am used to its length.

Pierce the piece to be appliqued from the WRONG side so that the needle exits the cloth on the right side of the fabric at the precise intersection of the two lines that form the upper right hand corner.

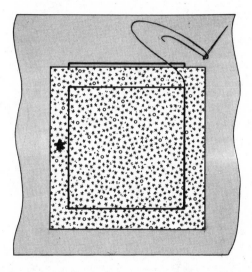

The needle exits the RIGHT side of the piece to be appliqued, in the upper right-hand corner. (p. 139)

Now, working from the right side of the fabric, and moving from right to left, take one small stitch in the BACKGROUND FABRIC, inserting the needle at the corner and having it exit on the sewing line one stitch length away. The needle should only pass through the background fabric.

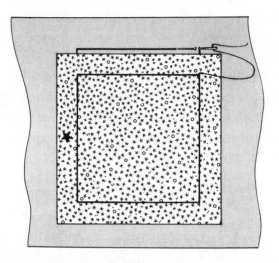

Take one small stitch in the BACKGROUND. (p. 140)

Next, take a stitch in the PIECE TO BE AP-
PLIQUED.

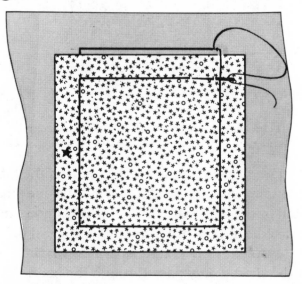

And another in the PIECE TO BE APPLIQUED. (p. 140)

   Insert the needle exactly opposite the point
from which the thread from the last stitch exits
the background fabric, and pass the needle only
through the piece to be appliqued.
   Take several more stitches alternating between the piece to be appliqued and the background. The path of the thread should look like
this:

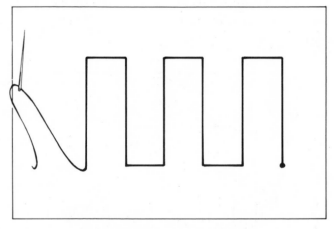

The path of the thread. (p. 141)

   Take care not to catch the seam allowance of
the piece to be appliqued. As you pull each
stitch, pull only enough to take up most of the
slack. Do not pull so hard as to disturb the
placement of the two pieces of fabric.
   Stitches should be small and even, about 10
to the inch. Stay on the sewing lines and space
your stitches evenly. Remember to insert the
needle precisely OPPOSITE the point from which
the thread is exiting from the last stitch.

At this point the mess you're holding in your hands makes you wonder why you ever bought this book. Understandable. With each "stitch" you are adding another parallel line of thread, another "toehooker." And so far it doesn't look a thing like applique. Wait. Trust me.

When you have taken enough stitches to count six parallel threads, stop. The thread should be coming out of the piece to be appliqued. More on that in a moment. Now comes the fun.

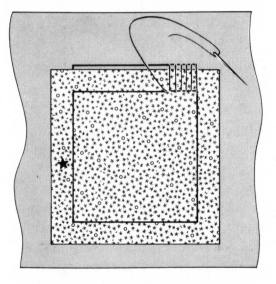

Six parallel threads are showing. (p. 141)

With the tip of your needle, or your fingers, gently roll under the seam allowance and pull the thread taut. Not only will the applique lay perfectly flat, but the thread will disappear!

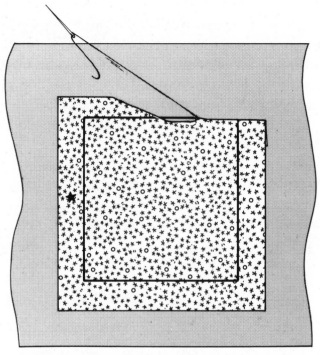

The thread disappears! (p. 142)

To make sure that you have not pulled the thread too tight, take the thumb and index finger of your non-needle-holding hand, and slide them along the fabric (both pieces) at the sewing line in the direction you are sewing. This will relax any excess tension.

If at all possible, try to take the last stitch of a series in the piece to be appliqued. Since it is nearly impossible to tell where the thread is coming from once the thread is pulled taut, knowing that you always take the last stitch in the piece to be appliqued can cut down on confusion.

At times, however, it will be more convenient to take the last stitch in the background. That's okay. Just remember what you did and be sure to take the next stitch in the OTHER piece. If you forget and take your next stitch in the wrong piece of fabric, you will have a skipped stitch.

Before continuing to sew, line up the sewing lines at the next easily recognizable point (the next corner) and pin beyond the sewing lines in the seam allowance. This will hold everything in place and give you something to aim for. The pin can be removed as you approach the corner.

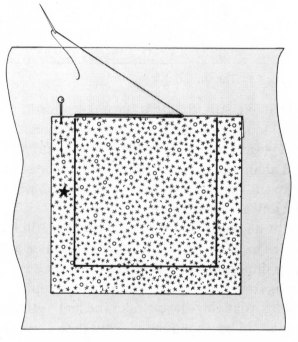

Pin in the seam allowance. (p. 142)

Then, simply pick up where you left off, alternating each stitch between the background and
the piece to be appliqued. After about 6 or 8
stitches, pull the thread taut again.

You will notice that using a pin to anchor the
next corner and the action of pulling the thread
tight will draw the applique piece right to the
sewing line on the background, thus obscuring
it. In order to see both sewing lines, you will
need to gently nudge the piece to be appliqued
away from the background. Use the thumb of
your non-needle-holding hand to do this.

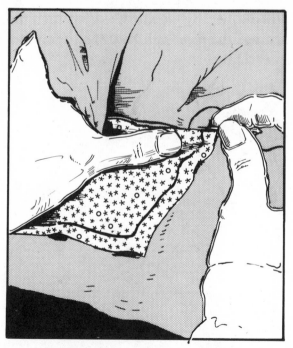

The thumb helps to expose the
background sewing line. (p. 143)

Use the tip of your needle to gently ROLL the seam allowance under as you sew. Never crush it flat, as your needle must enter and exit the sewing line easily without catching fabric on either side. Your needle should parallel the sewing lines as each stitch is taken. This is very different from traditional applique where it is necessary to finger press or even baste the seam allowance under and stitches are then taken at an angle.

To pull the thread without skipping a beat, anchor the thread already pulled taut with the thumbnail of the left hand. This way you will not pull all the way back to the knot each time. Then, cross the right hand over the left and pull the thread taut.

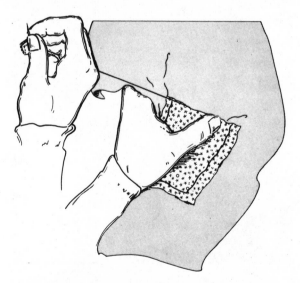

Cross the right hand over and pull. (p. 143)

Beginners should check constantly to see that the needle is inserted in one piece of fabric exactly OPPOSITE the point from which the thread of the last stitch has exited the other. It may help to touch the thread from the previous stitch with the point of the needle before inserting it into the next piece. Stitches should be the same length and the same distance apart.

Periodically, pull the piece to be appliqued away from the background after the thread has been drawn taut. Look at the stitches you have made. If you are proceeding correctly, the threads will be straight up and down. If you are not inserting the needle in the correct place, the stitches will appear to be V- or W- shaped.

It is a good idea to check the back as well. Stitches should be consistent, even, and small. If you can wiggle them with your fingernail, they are too loose. Pull the thread a little tighter.

As you approach the first corner, you may remove the pin you placed in the seam allowance earlier. Chances are it has done its job by the time it gets in your way. Remember not to sew past the marked lines.

After you have put in the last stitch in the first side, (in either the background or the piece to be appliqued) gently fold under the seam allowance of the second side. Then, turn your work so that the second side is on top, and continue sewing. Corners with a 90 degree angle or more need not be trimmed.

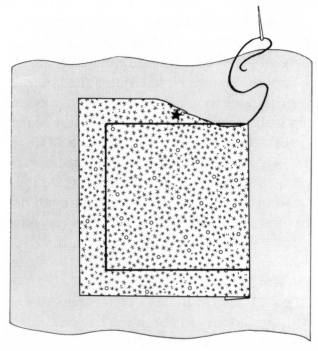

Turn under the next side and continue sewing. (p. 144)

Place a pin in the next corner, and check
periodically to see that your work is laying
flat.

When all four sides have been sewn, push
the needle through the background, turn your
work over, and knot off near the line of stitching. I like to catch a little bit of fabric with each
knot. One knot probably won't hold. Two knots
should do the trick. I put three knots in projects
I really like. Four knots, and you are beginning
to exhibit compulsive behavior! After knotting,
the background fabric can be clipped away, if
desired.

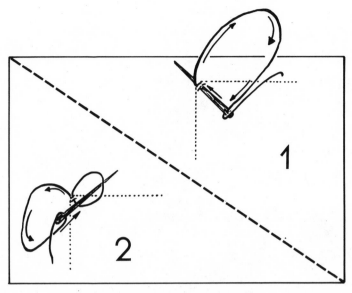

Knot off near the line of stitching. (p. 144)

CHAPTER III
CONCAVE AND CONVEX CURVES

The next illustration shows the rather odd shape for your next template. Prepare your template as before, although it will not be necessary to put an Orientation Mark along one side. It is not likely you will mistakenly turn this template the wrong way. DO, however, put a mark to designate right and wrong sides.

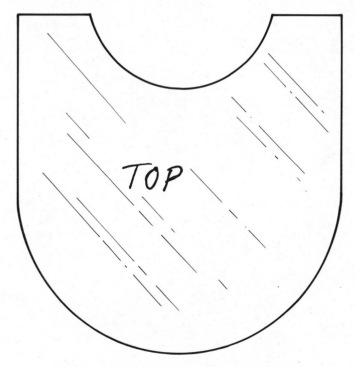

Template for concave and convex curves.

Align both pieces of fabric so that the grain-line runs vertically, and trace around.

In order to get the concave curve (inside curve) to lay flat, it is necessary to clip it. With a short, sharp pair of scissors, snip the entire curve, with clips running very close together, about every 1/4 inch or so. This will allow the seam allowance to turn under easily. Use the points of the scissors so that you can see when to stop, about 1/32 of an inch from the sewing line. Clip just before you are ready to sew to min-imize fraying. Convex curves (outside) need not be clipped.

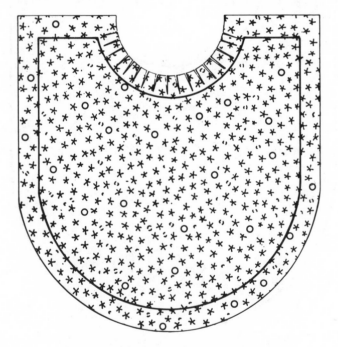

Clip concave curves closely.

Again, as with the square, there are four easily recognizable points from which to start. They are the left and right inside corners which enclose the concave (inside) curve, and the left and right outside corners which enclose the convex (outside) curve.

Since the inside curve is the one most likely to give you fits, do it first. Besides, it is much easier to correct alignment mishaps on the outside curve than it is on the inside curve, because the outside curve is longer. To make life just a little easier, begin sewing this shape with the straight line just before the inside curve. You're already a whiz at straight lines from working through the last exercise, right?

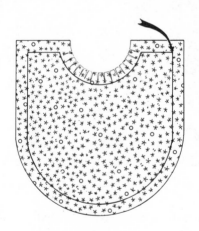

Begin here. (p. 145)

To begin, instead of making a series of parallel threads as you did before, start sewing in this manner: insert the needle in the corner of the piece to be appliqued from the wrong side of the fabric, as you did with the square. Now, gently roll under the seam allowance and bring the sewing line of the piece to be appliqued up to the sewing line of the background fabric. Continue sewing as before.

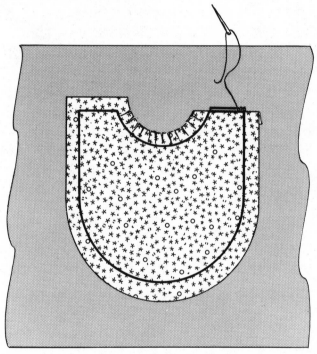

Roll under the seam allowance and begin sewing. (p. 145)

After two or three stitches, pull the thread taut. Locate the next easily recognizable point (the beginning of the curve) and pin. If the pin gets in the way, take it out and move it to the NEXT easily recognizable point, the end of the curve, or in the corner beyond.

Unless you have more than the normal com-
plement of fingers, it is futile to try and turn
under the entire seam allowance before you sew.
Just worry about the quarter inch of fabric
ahead of your needle, and learn to turn that
under with the tip of your needle.

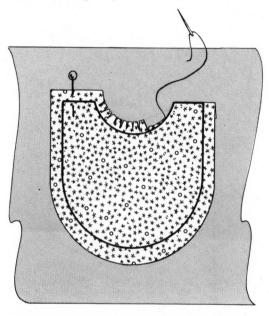

Turn under the seam allowance 1/4 inch at a time. (p. 146)

Don't cheat when sewing the inside curve.
Nudge the fabric back with your thumb so that
the sewing line is not obscured, and stick to it!

Remember to keep the stitches even, beginning each one exactly opposite the place where
the thread exited from the last stitch. If you
place each stitch opposite the last, the curve will
lay flat.

The same rules apply to the outside curve. Turn just a portion of the seam allowance under as you sew. Here you may wish to use another pin halfway along to keep the fabrics together since it is such a long distance. Stay on the sewing lines, and place your needle opposite the exiting thread of the last stitch.

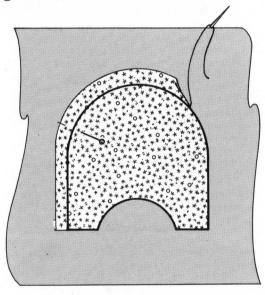

Sewing the outside curve. (p. 146)

CHAPTER IV
POINTS AND V-SHAPES

Prepare the next template and fabric as you have before, and, just for fun, thread your needle with thread that matches the piece to be appliqued!

A heart will give you practice with points and V-shapes.

It will also be necessary to clip the V-shape at the top of the heart. Notice that the center clip has also been clipped. This extra step helps the fabric to bend just slightly more for easier sewing.

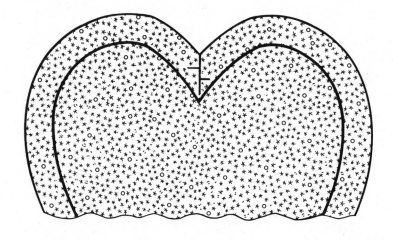

The heart shape must be clipped.

Although there are two easily recognizable points from which to start sewing the heart, the bottom point, and the base of the V-shape on top, begin sewing at the bottom of the heart. After a few stitches, match the sewing lines of the V-shape part of the heart on the piece to be appliqued and on the background, and pin it to hold it in place. Do not put the pin in the V-shape as the clipped heart is fragile enough as it is, especially at that point. Instead, pin beyond it.

Continue sewing up from the bottom of the heart and stop at the top of the first "bump." Now, fold under the second "bump" and trick the V-shape into thinking it is a straight line!

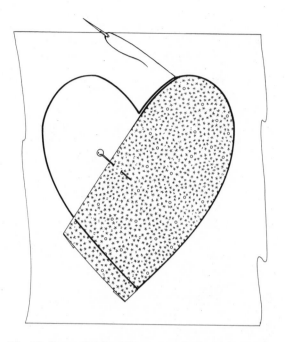

The V-shape thinks it's a straight line. (p. 147)

Sew to the bottom of the V-shape, but do not go beyond the sewing line. Then, coax the second "bump" of the heart up until the sewing line is visible. Since you have already sewn half of the V, fraying will be minimized.

As you come down again, toward the point of the heart, clip away any seam allowance that may be showing from the first side, and continue sewing.

For very acute points, trim the seam allowance to a narrower width near the point before you begin to sew.

CHAPTER V
CIRCLES

Below are an assortment of circular shapes, ranging in difficulty from "No Problem" to "You've Got To Be Kidding!" Start with the largest one.

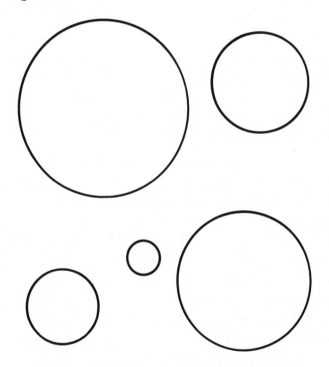

Start with the largest circle.

Prepare templates and fabrics as before. For the larger circles it will be helpful to add three Orientation Lines to help in placement and to give yourself something to aim for.

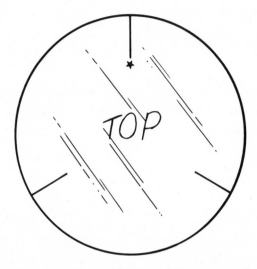

Orientation Lines will help position the circles
and give you a line to aim for.

Put a star by one of the Orientation Lines, to
tell it from the other two, and transfer it to both
pieces of fabric for easy alignment. For the
smaller circles it is better to mark just one
Orientation Line, as you probably won't have
room for much more. For very small circles,
wing it. You'll have a hard enough time just
holding on to the fabric.

When marking Orientation Lines from the
template to the fabric, it may help to trace over
the Orientation Line on the template and let
your marking tool run off the template and onto
the fabric.

One pin through the center of the circle will
be helpful. Make sure the circle lays flat as you
sew.

CHAPTER VI
COMMON PITFALLS

What went wrong? If your pieces are not matching up or laying flat consider these common problems:

- Improperly placed templates. Make sure you can tell the right side from the wrong side before you trace around each template, especially with shapes that appear to be symmetrical, but really aren't.

- Messy marking. Sewing lines must be as accurate as possible. Keep chalk pencils consistently sharpened from line to line. Avoid sketchy lines which are thick in some places and thin in others. Make sure all points and corners are complete and accurately drawn. Also, if you have to use two different marking instruments for each piece of fabric (pencil and chalk, for example) compensate for the thicker chalk line.

- Inconsistent grainline. It does make a difference. If the grainline of the piece to be appliqued is going in one direction, and the grainline of the background is going in another direction, they will not handle the same way. Each piece to be appliqued, depending on its position on the design field, may very well have its own place on the background fabric. Few if any pieces will be interchangeable.

- Uneven stitching. If the stitches in the piece to be appliqued are longer and farther apart than those stitches in the background, your applique will pucker or bunch. If the stitches in the background are longer and farther apart, you'll run out of background before the piece to be appliqued is completely sewn on.

- Using non-compatible fabrics. Whenever possible choose fabrics of the same weight. Sewing silk to denim can surely be done with this stitch, but, let's be practical, you're

asking for trouble, especially if it's your first
time out.

- Accidentally catching the seam allowance.
  This can give a rather bumpy appearance to
  your applique. Take care NOT to crush the
  seam allowance as you hold your work, or
  worse yet make an effort to press it under
  before you sew. If it is "rolled" under instead,
  you will be far less likely to catch it.

- Using bias strips for stems and vines. (This
  "easy way out" isn't.) Bias strips are hard to
  work with and don't always lay flat. Severe
  inside curves can pucker almost to the point
  of pleating, and always need to be sewn first.
  Outside curves stretched too far can pull
  your whole piece out of whack. Make a template for stems and vines, just as you would
  for any other shape.

- Shadow through. Dark fabrics showing
  through lighter ones appliqued over them is
  annoying. Clipping out dark backgrounds
  from behind and grading the seam allowance
  will help, as will lining the lighter piece to be
  appliqued.

- Ignoring the sewing line. You must enter and
  exit on the sewing line. Make sure you can
  see the lines and STAY ON THEM! If you

don't, you won't come out even.

When things are just a little off and your
sewing lines aren't matching up it is legal to
"fudge." Pin at the next easily recognizable
point, and ignore the sewing line on the background fabric until you can pick it up again.
You may have to "adjust" further if the next recognizable point cannot be matched because you
"fixed" something earlier.

If your lines matched up all the way around,
but the piece that has been appliqued appears
to be smaller than the background, giving it a
dented look, try sewing just inside the background sewing line next time. Sew on the bottom of the line instead of in the middle.
Changing needle placement by just a few
threads one way or the other should solve this
problem. Trimming the background may also
relax the piece that has been appliqued, and will
allow the batting to puff out the design when
quilted.

And, you should also know that with ALL applique, even traditional applique, the more
severe the shape the more difficult the fabric is
to handle. With that in mind, it's not a bad idea
to change a line here, broaden a point there,
and make life a little easier. This is a very good
idea, especially when faced with a beautiful pattern that will surely drive you nuts if you don't.

CHAPTER VII
PRACTICE

Well, there you have the basics. The preceding exercises should have given you practice in every shape you're likely to encounter in even the most sophisticated applique project.

If your stitches at this point still seem deliberate and awkward, give it a little time. After a few hours of practice (or a king-size Rose of Sharon) forming each stitch will be second nature to you. In just a short amount of time, you will be able to sew with ease and confidence.

Feeling confident already? Want to explore other ways to use Invisible Applique? Read on...

PART TWO:
OTHER APPLICATIONS

There's more to applique than layered block designs. Don't get me wrong, although I'm a sucker for vines, leaves, hearts, and tulips, and have been known to weep in ecstasy over a blurry photograph of a Baltimore Bride's Quilt, applique can take other shapes too. Repeating one patches, folded and cut whole cloth appliques, and picture quilts are but a few. In fact, ANY quilt that can be constructed using a traditional applique stitch can be made with Invisible Applique. And, for most of us, the results will look better, with less effort.

In this part of the book, I'll show you several projects in which Invisible Applique can be used instead of traditional applique. Some you've probably already thought of, others may not come immediately to mind. In each case I have my students to thank. Invariably, during each applique workshop I teach, someone always wonders aloud, "Hey, couldn't you use this stitch to.....?" Yes, you can.

CHAPTER VIII
CLAMSHELLS

If you get your jollies wrestling with curved seams, I suppose you could have a wonderful time *piecing* this one patch tessellation. There's probably even somebody out there who wants to do it on their sewing machine! Most of us, however, would probably rather applique it, and of those, a good percentage would consider sewing it to a muslin or background fabric for stability. I think there's a better way.

Sew each clamshell to the one above it, starting from the top and working your way down. Each patch will then contain both the piece to be appliqued (the outside curve along the top) AND the background (the inside curves and point along the bottom.) If you join the patches moving from the top to the bottom of the quilt, you will always be sewing simple outside curves.

Clamshell template with Orientation Line.

Transfer the clamshell template above to your favorite template material. Select your fabric and set it in front of you so that the grainline is running vertically. Trace around the clamshell template making sure to transfer the Orientation Line to the seam allowance of your fabric.

Sharp points have a tendency to get lost. It's hard to tell EXACTLY where they end. Measure the distance from the Orientation Line to the very tip of the clamshell. On this template it should be about 3 inches. Mark the cloth with a small dot at the very bottom of the clamshell so that when you are sewing, all the patches will be consistent and will fit together easily.

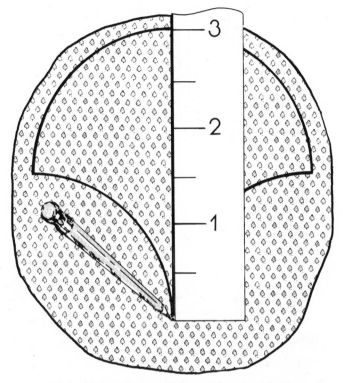

Put a dot at the very base of the clamshell.

When marking, be sure to leave extra room for seam allowances at the bottom of each clamshell. A good inch should be enough to extend the background so that you will have something to hold on to as you sew.

When you cut, leave the standard 1/4 inch around the top outside curve, and allow for the extended seam allowance around the bottom.

This may seem wasteful now, but it will make things easier in the long run. The excess seam allowance will be trimmed away later.

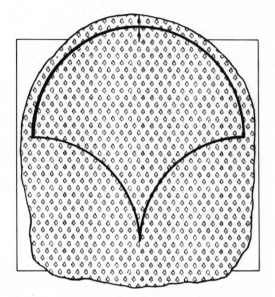

Leave ample seam allowance
at the bottom of each clamshell.

I find it makes most sense to start at the top
and work my way down to the bottom, building
each new row of clamshells on top of the row
above. In this way each clamshell is literally on
top of the one above it, and one can take advantage of only sewing convex (outside) curves. Construction also moves from right to left. (Left to
right for left-handed quilters.)

Begin each clamshell with five or six stitches
at the beginning of the outside curve. You may
wish to take the first stitch at a very *slight*
angle, having the needle enter the clamshell you
have just sewn, and exit in the clamshell above
it. This will tighten the point and give your work
a sharp, crisp appearance.

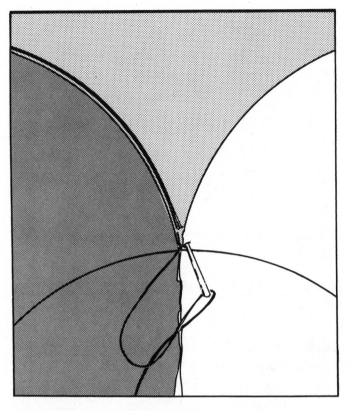

The first stitch enters the previously sewn clamshell, and exits in the clamshell above it. (p. 147)

After the thread is pulled taut, match the Orientation Line of the clamshell you are sewing with the spot where the clamshells directly above it meet. (This is also the bottom of the clamshell two rows up.) Pin.

On this long outside curve, it is important to have places along the way to aim for. Whether you roll the seam allowances under, or leave them out, don't forget to pin.

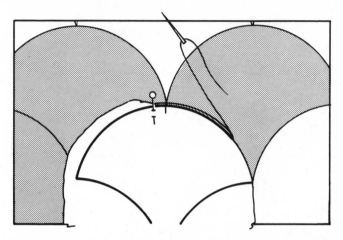

Match the Orientation Line and pin. (p. 148)

As you sew towards the pin, turn the seam allowance under with the tip of your needle. When you get to the pin, remove it, and match the end of the outside curve of the clamshell you are sewing with the point of the clamshell directly above it, and pin again.

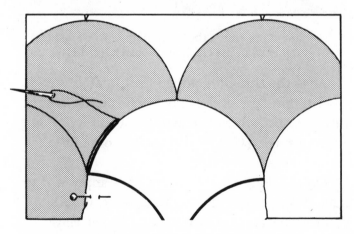

Match the end of the curve and pin. (p. 148)

Stop sewing at the end of the outside curve, turn your work over, and knot your thread. You may then trim the seam allowance of the background fabrics (the bottoms of the clamshells) to 1/4 inch so that it will match the seam allowance of the piece sewn to it. If this fabric is considerably darker than the clamshell sewn to it, grade the allowance so that it will not shadow through. You may wish to sew an entire row of clamshells before trimming to save time.

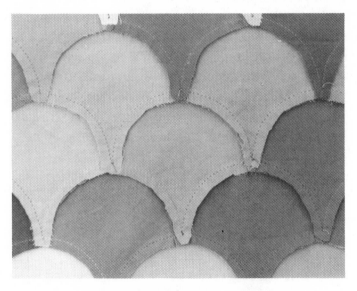

Wrong side of clamshells showing
seam allowances trimmed to 1/4 inch.

You may have noticed that I have cleverly avoided discussing templates for the very top of the quilt, the sides, and bottom, those portions made up of patches which are only parts of

clamshells. In order to make a quilt top with
straight sides, you will need to create filler
patches such as the ones used in the photograph at the beginning of the chapter. These can
be individual templates, created at the same
time as you draft your full clamshell, or they
can be full clamshells, partially sewn (i.e., only
the bottom half, only the side seam, only the top
curve) and trimmed straight after the quilt top is
complete.

If you elect to mark and sew full clamshells
and trim them later, plan to sew only as far as
you need to and no more. While I have no
qualms about lopping off patches mid-seam
when I machine piece, I don't recommend the
practice when hand sewing. To avoid raveling
you will have to go back and properly finish
hand sewn seam endings later, a tedious job at
best. Plan ahead.

To draft your own clamshell templates, make
a grid like the one pictured below. Place each
line at one half the length/width of your pro-
posed clamshell. (If you want a 4 inch clamshell,
each line on the grid should be 2 inches apart.)
Place one leg of the compass on point A, and
draw an arc from points B to C. Then place the
leg on point E, and draw an arc from B to D.
Next place the leg of the compass on point F,
and draw an arc from point D to C. The rest of
the grid will form the filler templates.

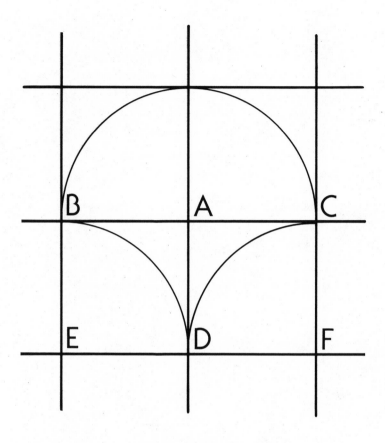

Drafting a clamshell.

CHAPTER IX
MOLAS

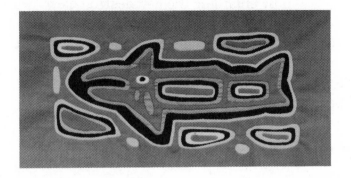

Although they are not quilted, and therefore technically cannot be considered quilts, *molas* are probably the most recognizable form of reverse applique. Originally made by the Cuna Indians of the San Blas region of Panama as front and back panels to adorn women's blouses (the blouses themselves are called *molas*) they have now found their way into the quilting world. Typically made in bright solid colors, *molas* often depict birds, fish and other wildlife. Though the lines are primitive and unsophisticated, eye-popping colors and intricate stitching brings this unique art form to life.

Each motif is surrounded by rings of rich bright colors built by layering cloth, and then cutting away and sewing one layer to the one beneath it. Smaller areas inside and between the central designs are embellished with rings of

applique. In some cases embroidery is also
added. The overall effect is one of complexity,
movement, and pulsating color.

Begin by enlarging the fish design below
to a workable size, (in this example, about
10 and 1/2 inches long) and then transferring it
to template material. Trace the design onto the
top and predominant color of the *mola*. This will
be your sewing line. In this example it is red.

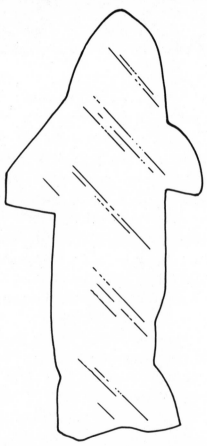

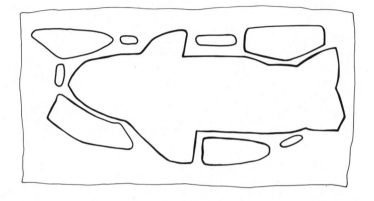

Trace the fish and add fillers.

Extend the *mola* to a rectangular shape by adding fillers. Draw rectangles, triangles and other shapes freehand, using the illustration at the beginning of the chapter as your guide. The lines you are drawing are sewing lines, and enough space must be left between them in order to turn under seam allowances. Keep in mind that the tighter the curve, the more difficult it is to sew. And, not all of them will be layered to expose multiple colors, so they can be as small as your confidence will allow.

Baste this top, red layer of cloth on top of the next color, in this case, orange. Grainline should be consistent in both pieces. Baste around the outside edge and again near the sewing line. This will keep the fabric from shifting and sliding while you cut and sew.

Baste carefully.

After you have basted, cut the top layer of cloth, about 1/8 inch from the inside of the sewing line. Save all of the cut-away fabric, even the little pieces, as they can be used later.

Cut the top layer of cloth.

Clip all inside curves, turn under seam allowances with the tip of your needle as you sew.
Because the fabrics are carefully basted, you
may start anywhere. It is impractical to use
Orientation Lines, as there is no sewing line
marked on the background. And, because there
is only one sewing line to follow (on the red fabric) make sure the seam allowance of the piece
to be appliqued is turned under far enough so
that the sewing line is at the very edge of the
rolled allowance. Place your needle directly
below it and into the orange background. Pull
the thread taut often and check frequently that
the applique is laying flat and smooth.

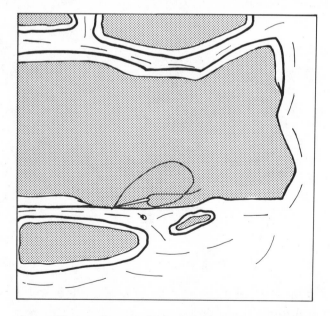

Insert the needle into the background directly below
the sewing line of the piece to be appliqued. (p. 149)

Sharp, tight, inside corners offer a particular headache in reverse applique. The more you fiddle with them, the more they will ravel and fray. The trick is to turn them with the tip of your needle on the first try, without accidentally catching the seam allowance as you take your stitch. Practice will help.

After all the areas on the top fabric have been sewn, mark the sewing line on the second (orange) layer, about 1/8 inch from the sewn edge of the top fabric. Mark only those areas large enough to accommodate another ring of color.

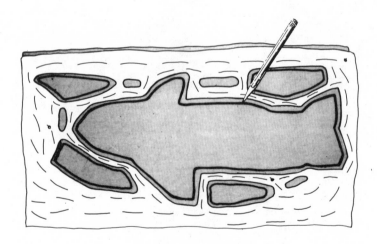

Mark the second layer.

Slip the third layer (black) under, keeping grainlines consistent, and baste again. Cut just inside the sewing line on the orange (second) layer, leaving 1/8 inch seam allowance. Clip inside curves, and sew.

When this third layer is in place, there is very little reverse applique left to do. The remaining rings of color are simply appliqued, with some small filler areas, such as the eye, done in reverse applique. The inside of the fish is made by taking the original fish template and cutting 1/2 inch off all the way around.

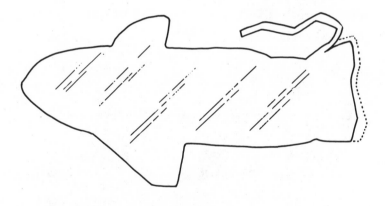

Cut 1/2 inch off the first template to make the second.

Now take this template and lay it on the red fabric cut-away you set aside earlier. Trace

around the template to create the sewing line,
baste the red fabric onto a piece of blue slightly
larger. Trim the seam allowances on the red fabric to 1/8 inch, and sew it in place, using applique around the outside edges and reverse
applique in the filler areas and eye. Again, save
the red cut-aways, as they will be used in the
filler areas later.

When this is done, mark the sewing line on
the blue fabric by drawing a line about 1/8 inch
from the sewn edge of the red layer. Baste the
red/blue layer onto the black, positioning it as
best you can in the center of the motif, and
baste. Turn under the seam allowance and applique around. You can think of it as one fish
framed in another.

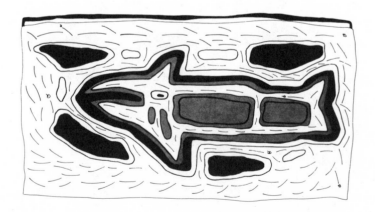

Sew one fish inside the other.

Mark, cut, and turn under the two blue filler areas inside the fish, and sew them to the black fabric beneath. Now take the red filler cutaways, and be brave. Without templates and without marking sewing lines, trim 1/8 inch all the way around to allow for another ring of color. Then, roll under 1/8 inch seam allowance and applique them to pieces of orange, green, pink, yellow, and/or blue fabric. These multicolor pieces should be at least 1/4 inch larger all the way around, and will be used to fill any leftover areas. (This is probably much closer to how "real" *molas* are made than all the previous fussing with sewing lines, and templates.) Then, take these units, trim them so that 1/8 inch seam allowance can be rolled under and still leave 1/8 inch of color showing, and applique these onto the black fabric to complete the *mola*.

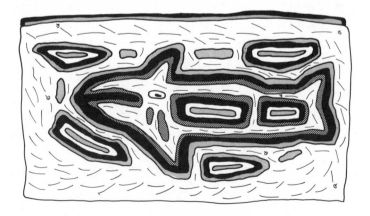

Multi-colored units complete the *mola*.

It is also possible to construct this *mola* by layering several layers at once, and cutting each away as needed. I didn't choose to present it that way for two reasons. First, knowing Murphy's Law as intimately as I do, if I layered more than I absolutely had to, I would probably poke the tip of my scissors through more layers than I had intended, and wind up slicing my *mola* to shreds. Second, with many layers handled and sewn at one time, stitches in the background might pass through multiple layers of cloth. While I suppose that's no great disadvantage, *I* find it awkward to catch more than a single layer. However, there's got to be more than one way to make a *mola.* Do what feels comfortable for YOU.

And, strange as *this* may sound, it is entirely possible to create this *mola* design without using reverse applique, although I'd call it something other than a *mola.* Each ring of color can simply be appliqued one on top of the other to achieve the pattern and color desired.

CHAPTER X
HAWAIIAN APPLIQUE

Hawaiian quilts are made by folding large pieces of paper, snow flake style. Elaborate curves and points representing stylized flora and fauna of the islands are then cut into them. The folded paper is placed on top of a large piece of fabric folded in the same manner, which is then cut. The resulting design is basted to a background of slightly larger proportions, and then appliqued by turning under the raw edge with the tip of the needle. Many times intricate borders are also added before the giant two color applique is meticulously "echo quilted." The effect is reminiscent of the ripples caused by a stone plunked into a still pond.

Even though no sewing lines are used, Hawaiian quilts *can* be sewn using Invisible Applique. Again, however, it must be remembered that the more severe the shape (the more acute the angles, and the deeper the curves) the more difficult ANY applique will be. And because no sewing lines are marked on the cloth, it offers a special challenge. Chicken-hearted quilters (like me) are encouraged to simply "pencil in" sewing lines 1/8 inch from the raw edge. I'll tell you when.

Begin by grabbing a piece of paper that is cut to a workable size. It does not necessarily have to be square, although the resulting applique motif will be. Fold it diagonally three times.

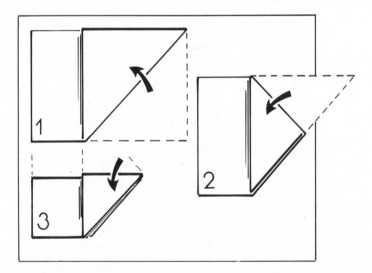

Hawaiian applique starts with a folded paper pattern.

When creating your own distinctive applique, it is a good idea to start with smaller pieces of paper, just to play around. When you think you've got a design you like, try it full size.

Leaving the point, and the folded sides partially intact, cut a curvy undulating design from the folded paper. Open it up, and if you have ONE design, instead of four parts, you've done well. If you have one you like well enough to transfer to cloth, enlarge it and continue with the next step.

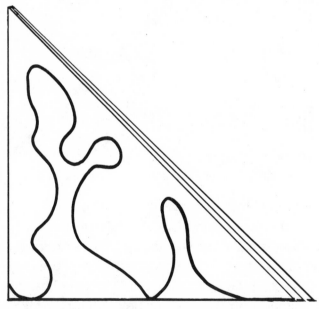

Cut the motif in paper first.

Next, iron the piece of fabric you will use to applique, and then fold it diagonally, just as you had prepared the paper earlier. Lay the folded

paper design on top of the folded cloth, and pin
it in place. Trace around the paper as if it were a
template, then remove it and cut along the
marked lines.

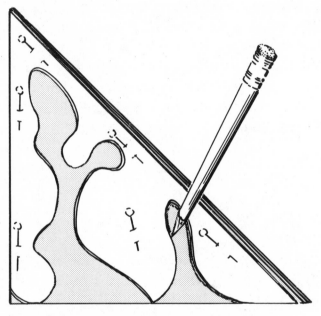

Mark the cloth using the paper as a guide.

Open the cloth carefully onto the background fabric, which has also been pressed.
Position it carefully so that grainlines are consistent, and smooth out all wrinkles. If the project is small (all of it fits on your ironing board at
one time), iron the piece to be appliqued onto
the background. The cotton fabrics will "stick"
and slide less as you baste.

Baste the two pieces together carefully.
Begin from the center and move toward the out-

side edges. Anchor every part of the design securely by basting 1/2 inch from *every* raw edge. Since there are no Orientation Lines to aim for, basting becomes very important, as does constant checking to see that everything is laying flat as you sew. It is better to over-baste than under-baste.

Since no guide lines are marked on the cloth, the rolled edge of the piece to be appliqued will serve as the sewing line. Placement of the needle on the background fabric should be immediately below the rolled edge of the top piece.

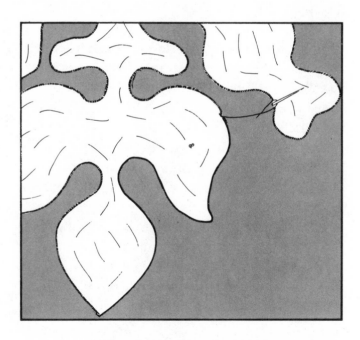

Place the needle in the fold,
and then directly below it. (p. 149)

If this drives you crazy, simply draw sewing lines 1/8 inch from the raw edge. Mark a foot or so at a time.

Start sewing anywhere you like, rolling the seam allowance under with the tip of your needle as you come to it. Clip inside curves as you approach them, but only if you are sure you will be able to sew them down before your current sewing session is over. If you clip and then let it go until another time, you run the risk of having the clips ravel before you even get to them.

If you will be working without sewing lines, you must take care to sew beyond the ends of the clips you've made. It's no fun to stick your needle through sliced fabric when you intended to catch a full piece. If you marked sewing lines, however, you'll have the added advantage of knowing exactly where your "clips" end, about 1/32 inch from the sewing line.

Again, very deep inside curves are tricky, and successfully rolling under seam allowances with the tip of your needle in very tight areas takes practice.

And, since there can be yards and yards of raw edges exposed in a Hawaiian applique design, take care to fold and unfold works in progress very carefully. Cut bias edges will ravel with very little provocation.

CHAPTER XI
STAINED GLASS

Stained glass windows are made by drafting a full-sized paper pattern, or cartoon, and then cutting it apart. Each piece is then glued to a piece of glass. The glass is cut to the shape of the paper pattern and the pieces of glass are fitted together to recreate the original design. Lead is then curved around the pieces to cover the sharp edges and to hold them in place, giving both structural and visual support.

Quilts made to resemble stained glass are usually made in much the same way. A full-sized paper pattern is drafted, then cut apart. Each shape is backed to make it stiff, and then used to transfer the pattern shape to cloth. The fabric is cut, and reassembled onto a background piece of fabric which acts as a foundation. Commercially cut and folded black bias tape, or home made bias strips, replaces the leading. It is manipulated, pinned, and then sewn over the raw edges. The results, like the windows from which they are inspired, are dazzling. Rich deep colors framed in black, give almost any design strength and vigor.

Using Invisible Applique will further emphasize the sharp contrast between the black "leading" and the colorful "glass." And, if you're willing to try an unorthodox method (or two) of making your stained glass quilts, I think the results will be even more spectacular.

Both methods are born out of my intense dislike for bias strips. The only time they should ever be used is as binding around the finished edge of a quilt, and then they should only be home made. Commercial bias binding looks store bought, and always draws attention to itself. The disadvantage of using bias strips in making stained glass quilts is two-fold, no pun intended. First, they are cut straight, and will only curve if you force them to. That means lots of pins, or lots of basting if you don't want your sewing thread snagged on one, or several, of the pins. Second, once the bias strips are pushed and shoved into position, the inside curves must be sewn first. That makes for frequent stops and starts when working on a line with more than one curve, which I find annoying and time consuming. Furthermore, inside curves sewn in this manner often look ribbed or wrinkly, and outside curves stretched too much can distort the entire piece.

There are two ways to avoid these pitfalls, and both methods begin with a full-sized paper pattern of your intended stained glass block. Draw it on tracing paper, first with pencil, and then with a thin felt tipped marker. Instead of imagining the black leading, as simply a wider version of your pattern lines, incorporate it into the paper pattern. Draw the leading a consistent 1/4 inch wide. Feel free to take the pattern below and enlarge it. In order to get the leading to measure 1/4 inch in width, the pattern should be just a smidge under 8 inches square.

Stained glass paper pattern.

Method A

Method A is closest to the real thing. The leading will be appliqued onto, or over, the glass background. It is the best way to achieve sharp points, but requires more marking, cutting, and sewing.

Begin by looking at the paper pattern above as if you were making it out of glass. Plan where each piece of leading will start and stop, and indicate on the paper pattern where overlapping will occur.

Same pattern, modified for Method A.

Labeling each pattern piece (letters for leading, numbers for glass) will help you keep track of them more easily once they are marked and cut.

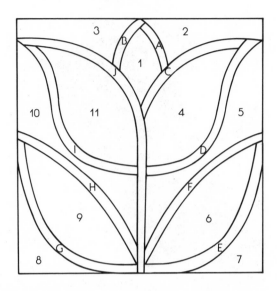

Letters and numbers are added for easy identification.

Use a lightbox to transfer each sewing line to fabric. If one is not available, the pattern may be cut apart and backed with sturdy template material or cardboard and traced around. Keep in mind however, that the more the pattern is transferred, the more chance there is for distortion. Cutting the pattern apart is one extra step that I urge you to try and eliminate, especially with very small pattern pieces such as the ones in this project.

As you trace the sewing lines onto the fabric, keep the grainlines consistent, and running vertically. It is also extremely helpful to mark little lines in the seam allowance to indicate precisely where one piece may meet or overlap another. These lines will be your only placement guides.

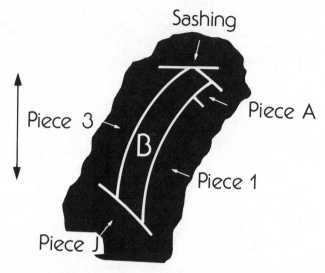

Each pattern piece should be labeled
and marked to reduce confusion.

When you cut, only 1/8 inch seam allowance
is necessary around the black (leading). Trim to
this width just before you are ready to sew to
minimize fraying. Leave at least an inch all the
way around the colors (glass) so that you will
have something to hang on to. You will clip
these seam allowances to match the others immediately after each seam is sewn. All inside
curves should be clipped just prior to sewing, as
well. About every 1/4 inch should do it.

Take some time before you begin sewing to
plan an assembly strategy. Think about the
order in which the seams should be sewn to
make best use of your time. Depending on how
you've charted a particular pattern, there may
be several ways to assemble the pieces.

The strategy outlined below represents the least amount of starting and stopping required to assemble the block above. Each seam, save one, is sewn in its entirety. There are, of course, many other ways to tackle this block. And, if you're like me, as soon as you commit yourself to one strategy, you're bound to find another one that you would have liked better.

Sew A to 1.
Sew B to 1A (A1).
Sew AB (BA) to 2.
Sew B to 3.
Sew C to 4.
Sew D to C4 (4C).
Sew DC (CD) to 2A1 (1A2).
Sew D to 5.
Sew E to 6.
Sew E to 7.
Sew F to 6E (E6).
Sew G to 8.
Sew G to 9.
Sew H to G9 (9G).
Sew H to 10.
Sew I to 11.
Sew J to I11 (11I), stopping (starting) at
    the intersection of I and 11 at the base of
    the flower.
Sew JI (IJ) to the long side of 10.
Sew the rest of J to 10HG (GH10).
Sew J to EF5D4C1B3 (3B1C4D5FE).

In the rather cryptic directions above, the
first unit identified should be treated as "the
piece to be appliqued," and it will be sewn to the
second unit which should be treated as the
"background." Units with multiple letter and/or
numbers are named by the order in which the
right-handed sewer will encounter them. Left-
handed sewers will see their version reversed
and in parentheses. Looking at your paper pattern will help, unless of course you've cut it up
to make your templates, in which case you'll
have to tape it back together again, or make
another one!

All sewing should be done with black thread
as this will match the leading, otherwise known
as the piece to be appliqued. Use the lines
you've marked in the seam allowance as your
guide. Match them up and pin whenever you
have the chance. On longer seams, where you
have no marks to aim for, you may wish to roll
the seam allowance under to position the sewing
lines exactly and pin the leading in place.

Stopping and starting on sharp angles can
be a little tricky. Only take a few stitches at a
time, pull the thread taut, and see if you've
matched all the sewing lines exactly. If so, continue. If not, cut the knot off, pull out your
stitches, and give it another try. Remember that
stitches should not catch the seam allowance.
Guide your needle only through the sewing
lines, not into the fabric below them.

Black borders or lattice stripping should be added to give the block a finished appearance. For Method A, I prefer mitered ones which are appliqued to the block (instead of the block edges being turned under and appliqued to the borders) because there are many seams coming together at the sides. By appliqueing the borders to the block, the seams will not have to be turned and the block will lay as flat as possible. Don't worry, miters will be discussed in Chapter XIII.

Pressing the completed block properly will also help in keeping it flat now and in quilting it later. Turn and fold the seam allowances under the black leading. If your allowances were neatly trimmed to 1/8 inch this will be only moderately difficult. If they are any wider, trim them now.

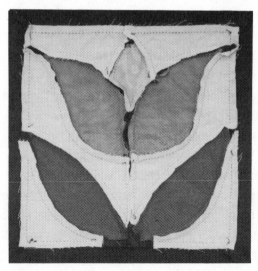

Wrong side of block, Method A, with seams pressed.

Press the wrong side first, then the right side, and only move the iron in an up and down motion. Never slide it across the block as this will undoubtedly catch the seams you've already pressed in the right direction and push them in the wrong direction. For stubborn seams and joins, basting the seam allowance in the proper position before pressing will help a great deal.

Once the seams are pressed and out of your way, quilting in the glass area just to the side of the leading will be much easier.

Method B

Method B is the imposter. In Method B, you will be doing the opposite of what you did in Method A. You will be appliqueing the glass to the lead. In the world of stained glass it is probably the equivalent of glueing the glass onto a sheet of lead. Tacky. In the quilting world, it is a little less shameful, but not much.

So why learn an "inferior" method? First of all, it's not inferior, just different. And second, although for some things it is not as precise, it IS about twice as fast and, for the beginner, is much less complicated than method A. Besides, if you're good at the stitch, unless you get your nose on top of it, the receding color of the lead will deceive your eyes and you'd swear you're looking at stained glass done The Correct Way.

Begin with the original pattern drawing at the beginning of the chapter, and don't change a thing. Transfer the sewing lines to the fabric representing the glass, making sure that grainlines are consistent, and running vertically. Cut them out leaving 1/8 to 1/4 inch seam allowance all around, and don't bother labeling them. You'll recognize their shapes easily and will know exactly where they go.

Then get a hold of a piece of black fabric the size of the block plus seam allowance. Since the black fabric will act as the background, transfer all the markings to it en mass. Those sewing lines running around the edge of the block can be sketched in, or forgotten, except for about a 1/2 inch from those places where appliqued pieces will start and stop. It is still helpful to have those lines for placement.

Prepare the black background.

Obviously, this technique works best when design dimensions are less than the standard fabric width of 44 inches. Seams in the leading would enable you to work a larger design, but might be visually distracting.

The assembly strategy for this second method is a piece of cake compared to Method A. You can start with any piece of fabric, and proceed in whatever order you like. Instead of 19 steps, you will have only 11.

As before, clip just before you are ready to sew, and remember to change the color of your thread to match the piece of glass you are sewing. Corners and points will be the places to aim for as you work around each piece of glass. Your headache will come if they are too sharp for your present skills. If they are, you've just discovered the only real drawback to this method.

When all the pieces have been sewn in place, very little pressing, if any, is required. The seam allowances have already been tucked under and positioned in the correct direction. You did that as you appliqued the glass in place. You may clip out the background, if you wish.

All that remains is to add a border to frame the block, and this can be done very simply, too. Go back to the original paper pattern, and transfer the outside lines, the square, to a piece of black fabric, making sure that the grainlines are consistent and vertical. (You could also just measure the finished size of the block and make a template that size, or measure it and transfer the square using a right angle and forget the template.) Trim the seam allowances around the square to 1/4 inch, match the corners of your block with the corners of the border piece, and begin appliqueing the block to the borders around it. Clip out the background under the block when you have finished.

Adding the borders.

With method B, your quilting strategy should be revised, since seam allowances are now directly under the area recommended for quilting with Method A. To miss those extra layers, simply quilt around the glass in the leading.

Wrong side of block, Method B, with seams pressed.

CHAPTER XII
PICTORIAL QUILTS

Pictorial quilts open up design possibilities which are limited only by one's own creativity and the restrictions of the fabric medium. Invisible Applique, more so than traditional applique, allows you to translate almost any picture into cloth. You'd be surprised at what is possible, and generally what isn't, can be, if the picture is enlarged so that the difficult part becomes big enough to hang on to and sew.

Although pictorial quilts can be created "on the run," sewing each piece to the quilt as inspiration hits, I encourage you to work with a paper cartoon or pattern. Draw the cartoon to scale on heavy white paper and place it over a lightbox to transfer the sewing lines to the fabric. There is much less ripping by doing it this

way, and after the pain of drawing the design,
all you have to worry about is fabric selection,
texture, contrast, and color as you mark and
sew.

Cartoon for pictorial seascape.

Another advantage in planning ahead is that
you will know, before you ever take needle to fabric, precisely how far each seam needs to be
sewn. The back can be clipped out after the
seam is sewn without any worry that there may,
or may not be, another piece of fabric placed on
top of it. Or worse yet, *under* it.

Using a cartoon doesn't mean that one can't
change one's mind. This is probably why I carry
around a 2-pound eraser, and buy correction
fluid by the gallon. If, as I proceed, I find that
certain lines are just too difficult to sew, I adjust
the cartoon and try again.

Using a cartoon will allow you to transfer sewing lines directly to the fabric, for precise placement of each piece. Furthermore, there is no need to work with a muslin, or a background fabric which has the entire design drawn onto it. While a muslin may provide a map to follow, it also adds another layer of cloth to quilt through, and is not very practical for designs with overlapping pieces built one on top of the other.

If working with a lightbox is too high-tech, the cartoon may be cut apart and glued to stiff template material and traced around. Doing it this way, however, is much more time consuming, and will make your job of fitting the pieces together more difficult. Each time you transfer a pattern, there is a greater chance for distortion. If your design has more than a few, very simple shapes, you should try the lightbox.

Storm Window, Trash Can, and Flashlight.

The not-so-high-tech lightbox.

The sewing strategy for pictorial quilts is fairly straightforward.

Begin at the top and work your way down towards the bottom, remembering that each piece of fabric will, at different times, act as the piece to be appliqued *and* as the background. When marking and cutting the fabric, leave ample seam allowances all around, so that when a particular piece is the background, you will have enough to hang on to. As in the other projects, grainlines should run vertically, and don't forget to mark those areas where other patches are sewn under or over the patch you are marking. These are sometimes the only guides you have while sewing. They are essential in that they give you something to aim for and to sew towards.

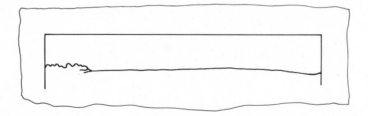

Sky patch marked with placement lines,
and cut with ample seam allowances.

For those pieces that will become part of the
four sides of the quilt top, leave at least 2 inches
along those outside edges, especially if it will
take a long time to complete the project. Better
to fray a healthy seam allowance as the work in
progress is folded and unfolded, than to risk
damaging the parts that will eventually show.
Don't forget to mark the outside boundaries of
the design as well as the sewing lines.

In the example above, begin with the sky fabric. The bottom edge becomes the background
as the first piece (the trees in the background) is
sewn to it. Since the tree patch is handled as
the piece to be appliqued, trim the top seam allowance to 1/4 inch, roll it under and begin to
sew. Right-handed sewers will begin at the right-
hand side, where the trees meet the water and
sky. Left-handed sewers will begin on the left-
hand side at the outside edge of the quilt.

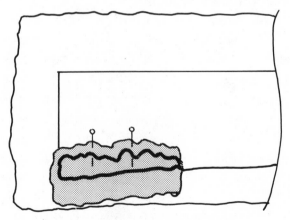

Sew the trees to the sky. (p. 150)

Do not sew past the end of the sewing line. It is not necessary, and might interfere with later seams. Immediately after the seam is sewn, turn your work over, knot off, and trim the seam allowance of the background to meet that of the piece to be appliqued.

Depending on the design of your quilt, and your expertise, you will be able to designate some seams as background, and some seams as piece to be appliqued before you even cut them out. In that case, feel free to trim those seam allowances to 1/4 inch. If you're wrong, it will just be difficult to hold on to as you sew. The beauty of Invisible Applique, is that even after a seam is sewn, you can tuck the seam allowance under the other piece if you change your mind. Provided you have not accidentally caught the seam allowance as you sewed, all the seam allowances are free and moveable. That is not the case with traditional applique.

To take advantage of difficult curves that might be sewn more easily as outside curves rather than inside curves (depending on which piece is the background, and which piece is the piece to be appliqued and your particular preference) it is perfectly legal to change the "top to bottom" sewing strategy, too. If you are at all concerned about the strength of the work, sewing outside curves might be preferable to sewing inside ones that need to be clipped often.

Generally, however, each piece is sewn on to

the one above it. In the seascape example, the trees are sewn to the sky, the shore to the trees, the water to the shore and sky, and lastly the near shore and rocks are sewn on to the water. After each piece is sewn, the seam allowance of the background it was sewn to is trimmed.

Wrong side of pictorial seascape.

Pictorial quilts are much like jig saw puzzles. The simple ones go together easily, and the more complicated ones are a bit more of a challenge. There are, however, some tricks. When working with lots of very small pieces (see *Neuschwanstein* on the back cover), look for the easy (sometimes the *only*) way out.

To get very sharp, inside corners, try layering. The battlement was made by first appliqueing the rectangles (crenels) onto the wall (background) behind it, and then putting a long narrow strip *over* them.

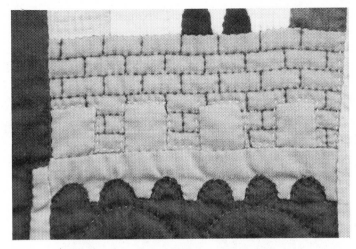

Crenels were sewn first, then the rest of
the battlement was sewn on top of them.

Very sharp points, especially those with two
or more different fabrics coming together, are
nearly impossible when the quilt is this small. I
did the best I could and embroidered the rest!

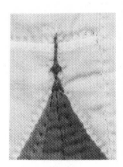

Matching embroidery floss helps draw out the point.

I also found my skills lacking when it came to appliqueing five pointed stars that measure a measly 3/8 inch from point to point. I resorted instead to permanent ink!

Permanent ink is permissible, too. Test it first.

CHAPTER XIII
MORE APPLICATIONS

Mitering

Perfect miters in borders, sashes, and bindings can be sewn using Invisible Applique. Working from the right side of the fabric, you'll see immediately if you've done it correctly. You don't have to wait until you've completed the seam, flipped it over, and found you were off.

Using a mitered border as the example, cut out the borders to the desired length (plus some, for safety) and the desired width (plus 1/4 inch, for seam allowance) Mark the sewing line on the borders. They should already have been marked on the quilt top. Applique the borders onto the quilt top. Do not sew beyond the ends of the sewing lines, and press.

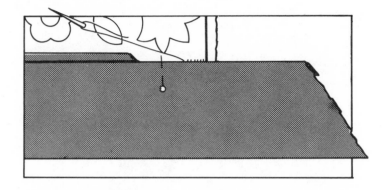

Applique the borders to the quilt top. Press. (p. 150)

Fold one border over the other, forming a right angle. If the borders are of consistent width, and cut straight, the fabric beyond the fold will run parallel to the border underneath it.

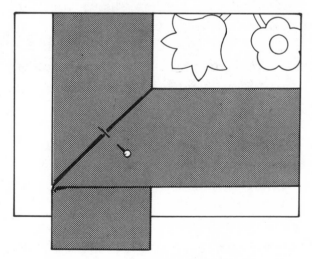

Fold one border over the other. Pin in place. (p. 151)

Hold the work so that folded edge is at 12 o'clock. Insert your needle into the background, at the corner of the quilt top, from the wrong side. (It's just too hard to fish the needle under the fold and burry the knot in the piece to be appliqued.) Applique as usual.

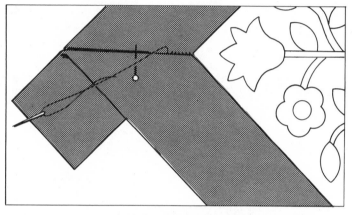

Applique as usual. (p. 151)

When the seam is complete, trim both the fold and the background. Press to one side.

Binding

Invisible Applique is an excellent way to sew down bindings, whether you use the square-corner or mitered-corner method. It will finish off your quilt with a sharp, smooth, sewn edge.

Use your sewing machine to attach the binding to the quilt as you normally would. Fold the binding over to the back, and tuck in the raw edges. The fold of the binding acts as your

sewing line, and the quilt back, just beyond the
line of machine stitching used to attach the
binding to the quilt, acts as your background
line. Pin to hold everything in place.

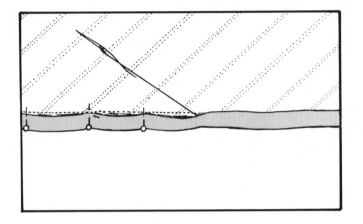

Applique the binding to the quilt. (p. 152)

Making Repairs

Although I would rather live with a quilt that
has a small blemish or two (or three or four)
before I try to repair it and possibly risk com-
promising the integrity of the quilt, simple re-
pairs can be made using Invisible Applique.

If you can take a measurement and create a
template from another block in the quilt, do so.
The marked sewing lines on the replacement
patch will help. If not, cut your replacement
patch a little larger than you think you should,
and fold under the raw edges. Begin at one of

the corners and applique the new patch right over the old one, quilting lines and all. Obviously, the new patch will be the piece to be appliqued, and the fold will be your sewing line if you are template-less.

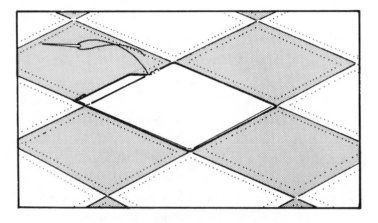

A new patch is appliqued over the old. (p. 152)

If the gods are smiling, the seam allowances of the old quilt won't be tucked under the patch you're replacing. That makes things a little more tricky. If they are tucked under the patches on either side, it will be easier to catch the fabric of the background without catching anything else.

Once the applique is done, you can either make the quilt look pretty from the top, or make it look pretty from the top and the back but also weaken the quilting.

If you elect to make it look nice only on the top, quilt over the new patch and leave the original quilting alone. If you want it to look good from the back as well, carefully rip out the original quilting from the back before re-quilting. If you can, pull the quilting stitches out and knot the ends of the threads and bury them to keep the quilting from coming undone in other places. Since you don't know the quilting strategy the original quilter took, and threads are fragile, you're playing a dangerous game here.

If you are determined to have the quilt look pretty from both sides and are handy with a needle, try quilting over the new patch without catching the backing or lining of the quilt. Sew just through the new patch, the old patch, or what is left of it, and the batting. Quilting just inside, or just outside, the original quilting should help.

Little Extras

OK, so this has nothing to do with quilting, but as I said before, Invisible Applique is an incredibly versatile stitch. It's not only terrific for all kinds of applique, miters, binding, and repairing old quilts, it is a great way to do some other things, too.

If you're a quilter, chances are you've dabbled in other kinds of sewing as well, like making stuffed animals. Or at least fixing ripped seams in stuffed animals made by somebody else? Next time you're sewing up the back end of some Teddy Bear, try Invisible Applique instead of a whip stitch.

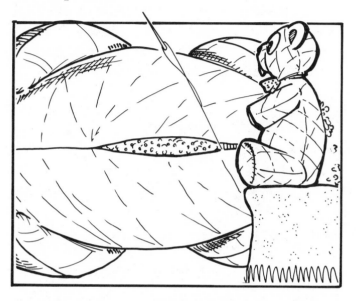

Bear repair using Invisible Applique. (p. 153)

Do you have furniture? Sure you do. Construction methods, small children, and luck being what they are, you may get a split seam from time to time. Repair it with Invisible Applique.

And, just one more. Would you like to put a small narrow hem on a scarf? Thanks to a former student, I've learned it's the same stitch, with a little variation. Instead of having the length of each stitch equal the space between them, try a long stitch in the piece to be appliqued and a regular size stitch in the background.

To turn the hem, fold the raw edge up 1/4 inch. The bottom fold is the piece to be appliqued. Imagine a sewing line in the background, just above the raw edge. Take several stitches as shown below, and pull. You'll get a beautiful rolled hem about 1/8 inch wide.

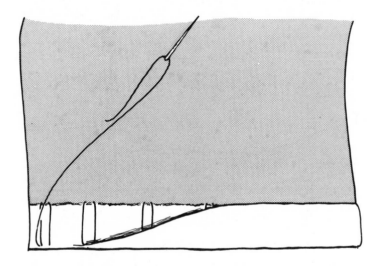

Making a rolled hem. (p. 153)

PART THREE: PIECING

And now, for the ultimate in applique: hand piecing. Why not? It's just a different means to the same end. Your finished blocks will look exactly as if they had been hand pieced, right down to the running stitch on the back. No one will be able to tell the difference.

So if it looks exactly the same, why bother?! Simple. Piecing with Invisible Applique allows you to see both sewing lines *at the same time*! You won't have to constantly flip your work over to check if you're on the line. You'll already know. Since you align sewing lines and pin from the top, you won't accidentally spear yourself with pins you've meticulously sunk through corners to match up your sewing lines. You'll be able to see that corners match (or maybe don't match) *as you sew them*, not after you're past them and it's too late.

Complicated blocks with set in patches that used to be impossible to sew without adding an extra seam, clipping a corner, or growing a third arm won't even make you flinch, and curved seams will be a piece of cake.

The following chapters will start you off slowly with straight seam piecing and simple blocks. Then you'll move on to more complicated blocks, and curved seams. There won't be anything you can't do.

CHAPTER XIV
NINE-PATCH

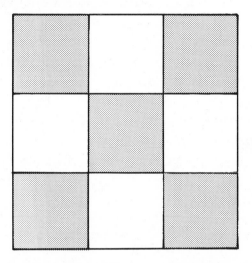

It's best to start with something easy. The end product is going to look very familiar, but getting there might be a little strange at first.

The template.

Begin with the square above, and transfer it
to your favorite template material. Assuming
that you are careful in making your template
(and it really is square) and because the strategy
in piecing is different than in applique, there is
no reason to bother with Orientation Marks.

There is cause, however, to pay attention to
grainline. As before, grainline must be consistent, and should run vertically. Now don't say
"Uh-huh," and keep reading. Take a pencil,
make a piecing diagram of your own, and draw
little grainline arrows. Indicate a vertical grainline arrow on *each and every patch.*

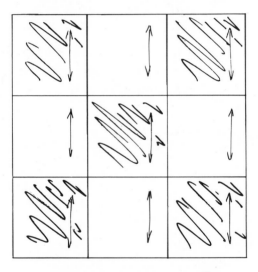

Grainline always runs vertically.

This is very different from the way most
people hand piece. Usually, the grainline is determined by the shape of the patch. Not so here.

You may, depending on how you were taught to hand piece, now have an overwhelming urge to mark little arrows on your template as well. Control yourself. While it won't matter on a Nine-Patch, it will definitely confuse things on most every other block. Don't mark grainline arrows on your template. I'll let you mark them on something else in a moment.

Now select your fabric and lay it right side up in front of you so that the grainline is running vertically. By looking at the piecing diagram, determine how many squares of each fabric are needed for the Nine-Patch, and prepare to mark the fabric.

Traditional hand piecers would only leave 1/2 inch between marked sewing lines as they trace around the template. When they cut out their squares they would then get the standard 1/4 inch seam allowance and be done with it. Using Invisible Applique requires a much heftier seam allowance on some sides of some patches, allowing you to have a little more cloth to hang on to when these patches act as the background.

If, after trying the stitch to piece, you find 1/4 inch seam allowance is comfortable, or you are sufficiently adept at planning which seams need a small seam allowance and which seams need a larger one, then by all means allow whatever seam allowances you wish.

Right now, since this concept is probably as

clear as mud, don't discriminate, and leave at least an inch seam allowance on *all* sides. This means you'll have to spread out as you trace around the template. You will be using slightly more fabric than you are accustomed to. Think of it as an excuse to go out and buy more.

Plan ahead so that you can leave large seam allowances.

Now let yourself go, and mark little grainline arrows, or lines, in the seam allowance of each patch. Cut them out leaving the entire seam allowance you've planned for. (Try not to fall into old habits and accidentally whack off all the seam allowances to a neat 1/4 inch!)

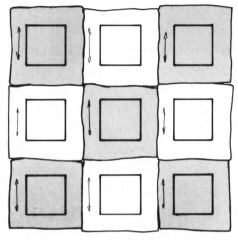

Grainline arrows are marked in the inch seam allowance.

After the patches have been marked and cut, lay them in front of you, right side up, grainlines vertical, according to the piecing diagram. Now you're ready to start sewing.

In patchwork, it is an accepted practice to press finished seams to the darkest side. That is, the seam allowances rest under the patch of the darkest color, and not under the patch of the lighter color where it might be slightly visible and then detract from the appearance of the quilt. If both patches are of equal value, and read the same, one arbitrarily decides under which color patch the seam allowances will rest, and then sticks to it.

Because it is a time-honored tradition to press to the dark side, and because it makes sense, we will adopt the following convention:

For each seam, treat the dark patch as the

piece to be appliqued, and the light patch as the background.

As you applique each seam, the seam allowance is rolled under the darker fabric. It is already in the right place. Chances are good that little more pressing will be required, as the handling it receives as you stitch will "finger press" the seam allowance in place. Furthermore, you will be working with a safety net.

Ideally, when using this stitch to hand piece, the seam allowances are free. You can move them at will to whatever side you wish. If, however, you accidentally catch the seam allowance when stitching, it loses this important property. If you designate where the seam allowance is to go *before* you sew, should you inadvertently catch the allowance with your needle, rendering it immobile, you won't have to worry. It's already "stuck" under the correct patch, the dark one. Keeping seams consistently under the dark patches will also help in "notching" (matching corners) later on.

If, however, you are sewing a particular block, and for ease of construction, it would make most sense to tuck the seam allowance under the light patch, go ahead. More on this in later chapters.

So, look at the piecing diagram below. Patches 1, 3, 5, 7, and 9 are dark, and would be appliqued to patches 2, 4, 6, and 8, which are light. Here's the assembly strategy:

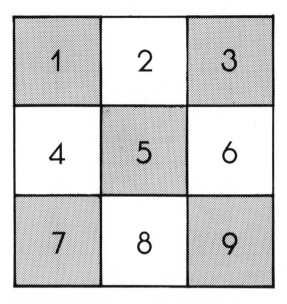

A) Applique patch 1 to patch 4.
B) Applique patch 7 to patch 4.
C) Applique patch 5 to patch 2.
D) Applique patch 5 to patch 8.
E) Applique patch 3 to patch 6.
F) Applique patch 9 to patch 6.
G) Applique strip 1-4-7 to strip 2-5-8.
H) Applique strip 3-6-9 to strip 2-5-8.

Since all this is pretty strange, let me walk
you through it step by step.

First find patches 1 and 4. Patch 1 is dark.
Trim the bottom seam allowance of patch 1 to
1/4 inch, role it under, and pin patch 1 to patch
4. Sewing lines of the seam involved should be
exposed, corners should be lined up, and the
pin should be in the seam allowance.

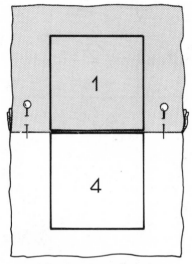

Patch 1 pinned to patch 4.

You will notice that the 12 o'clock orientation is now up-side-down. Turn it around the
right way, and applique as usual.

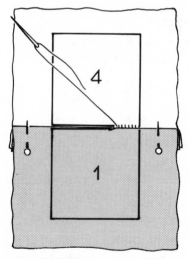

Begin to applique as usual. (p. 154)

Sew to the end of the lines and not beyond.
After the seam is sewn, turn your work over,
knot off, and trim the other seam allowance
(patch 4, which has acted as the background) to
1/4 inch.

Put the two patches you have sewn back into
the arrangement in front of you. Check to see
that you've proceeded correctly. Then grab
patch 7, trim the top seam allowance to 1/4
inch, roll it under, and pin it to the bottom of
patch 4, and sew.

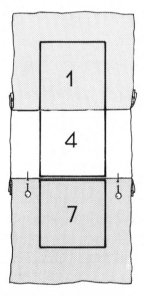

Patch 7 is appliqued to the other side of patch 4.

Notice that you did not have to turn your
work around. It was already in the 12 o'clock
position. Trim the remaining seam allowance
after the seam has been sewn, and proceed with

the other patches according to the assembly strategy above, until you have sewn three strips.

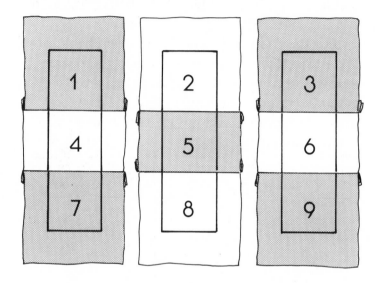

Applique the remaining patches into strips.

Set the strips in front of you, and admire your work. Grainline should be running vertically, and seams are free, yet tucked under the darker patches. (If they are not, tuck them in that direction and finger press them in place.)

In assembling strips 1-4-7, 2-5-8, and 3-6-9 to complete the nine-patch, follow the same dark-light strategy. Locate the strips with the most dark (1-4-7 and 3-6-9) and applique them to strip 2-5-8. Strips 1-4-7 and 3-6-9 become the piece to be appliqued while strip 2-5-8 becomes the background. Trim seam allowances of

strip 1-4-7 and 3-6-9 to 1/4 inch, and begin
sewing.

To assure that the corners meet precisely,
notch, or butt the previously sewn seams at the
corners. Since the seam allowances are under
the dark patches, making them slightly higher,
and because they alternate with the light
patches, which, by comparison, are slightly
lower, they will fit together easily. The slight vari-
ance in height will allow them to fit together
much like a puzzle. Pin beyond the corner, in
the seam allowance, and sew.

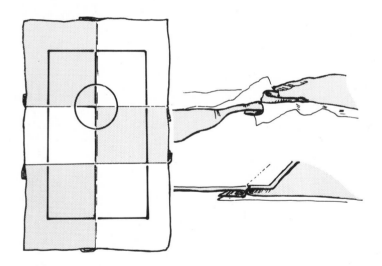

Notch or butt the corners and pin.

Trim the seam allowance of strip 2-5-8 to
1/4 inch after each seam is sewn, press and
your nine patch is complete.

CHAPTER XV
SUSANNAH'S PATCH

Begin Susannah's Patch by copying the block diagram above, and adding vertical grainline arrows to each patch. Then transfer the shapes below to template material.

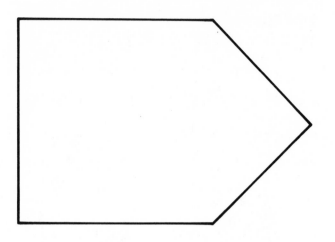

Leave ample seam allowances all around as you mark and cut, and note that half of the "house" shapes have the grainline running parallel to the short side, and half have the grainline running parallel to the long side. You will have to turn the template when marking. The large square, the one in the middle, is cut on the bias!

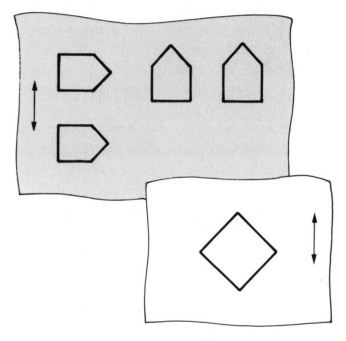

Keep the grainline consistent and running vertically.

If you are working with regularly patterned fabric, or for some reason wish to have printed or bordered fabric running a particular way within the block, remember that artistic placement of patterned fabric always outweighs grainline considerations.

In any case, mark grainline arrows in the seam allowances of each patch, just to keep everything straight, and lay them all out in front of you to plan your assembly strategy. As you pick up each piece to sew, check the grainline markings in the seam allowances to make sure you have the correct piece for that particular spot in the block.

In this block, like most blocks, there are several ways to proceed. You will want to observe the dark-light strategy, but even so, there are a few options. (And a few exceptions, but we'll tackle those in a moment.)

You could sew all the darks to all the mediums along the long seam, then join the four units along the short seam, and add the lights last. Or, you could sew the darks to the mediums at the short seams first, and then join those units at the long seam, adding the lights last. Or, you could sew the darks to the mediums, then to the lights, and then to one another. Or, you could sew dark to medium, then medium to dark, working your way around in a circle, and then add the lights last. Or, you could start by sewing a dark to a light, then the medium to the light, then the dark to the medium, and proceed quarter by quarter, saving the large light for last. Or, you could... Get the picture?

Just because you are using an applique stitch, and making a decision about where the seam allowance is going to be placed before you sew, doesn't mean you are narrowing your options.

My recommendation would be to assemble the block as you feel most comfortable, were you hand piecing that *other* way. In case you're new to that, too, let's try it like this:

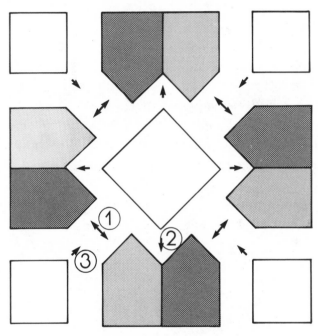

Assembly strategy.

Begin by sewing the darks to the mediums along the long side. Take these four units, and, appliqueing the darks to the mediums, join them together along the short side, making a donut. Applique the large center square *to* the darks and mediums, and then applique the four smaller squares in the corners to the rest of the block.

Now hold it, didn't she just say a few pages back to always applique the dark to the light, to tuck the seam allowances consistently under the darker fabric?! You can certainly do it that way, but remember I also said there could be exceptions from time to time? Here's one worth considering.

By saving the light squares for last and appliqueing them to the rest of the block (instead of vice versa), there is slightly less fiddling. And, the seam allowance placement, in this case, won't effect notching in the slightest way, because there are no corners to notch. Whichever strategy you select, however, be consistent. Don't sew three squares one way, and the fourth another, unless you plan on pressing the seam allowances to correct the discrepancy.

CHAPTER XVI
FARMER'S DAUGHTER

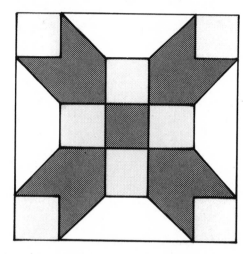

Begin as before, by creating a piecing diagram with grainline arrows marked on each patch, and by transferring the shapes below to template material.

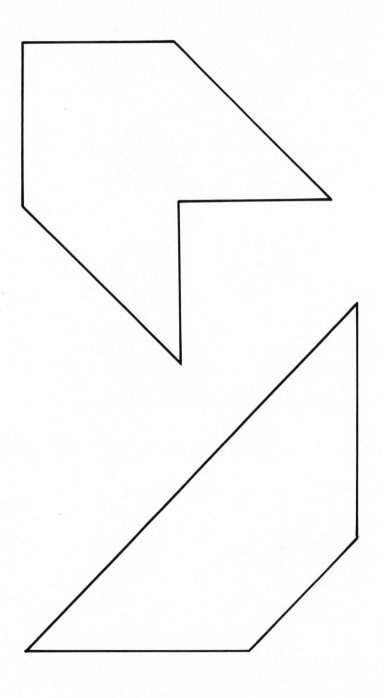

Mark and cut the fabric, making sure to leave ample seam allowances around all patches, especially around the chevron shape. Remember that two of the three templates will have to be turned when marking so that the grainline will run vertically in all patches. Mark the grainline of each piece in the seam allowances.

Again, as with all blocks, there are several approaches to consider. The most straightforward, however, is to treat the block as a "glorified" Nine-Patch, and assemble it accordingly.

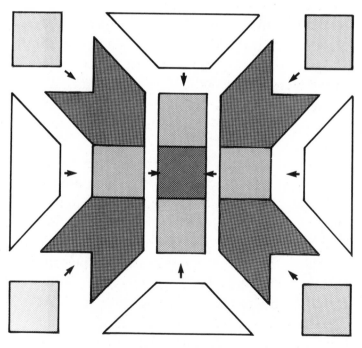

Assembly strategy.

Begin by imagining that the chevron shapes are merely the corners of a Nine-Patch, and sew the nine patches into three vertical strips. Then sew the strips together. The light "lopped-off triangle" shaped pieces along the outside edge of the block, and the medium squares at the four corners, will be appliqued to the block last.

Notice that you will be sewing the dark patches (piece to be appliqued) to the medium patches (background), placing the seam allowances under the darker of the two fabrics, until you sew the light patches and the four corners. At that juncture, you will ignore the dark-light strategy for several reasons.

First, while it is possible to sew the predominantly dark block *to* the light patches and the medium squares, it is easier to reverse the strategy and sew the light patches *to* the block, tucking the seam allowances of the chevron shape away from the points and not under them.

Second, in order to sew the chevron *to* the medium square, it would have to be treated as a V-shape. The base of the V would have to be clipped. Clipping weakens the fabric, and as long is it can be avoided, it should be.

Third, this is the Big Advantage to piecing with Invisible Applique. It offers you an alternative to traditional hand piecing where you would have to at best clip the chevron, at worst split the patch with another seam in order to set it in, and pivot in the middle of the seam in either case. By appliqueing the light patches and the medium corners *to* the block you will have achieved the desired result with minimal effort.

Best of all, you can adapt this same strategy to any block that ordinarily would require "setting in" patches, from a Bow Tie to a St. Louis Star. With Invisible Applique patches no longer have to be subdivided, and few, if any ever have to be clipped. Pivoting seams, and the acrobatics of holding on to pinned patches from the wrong side as you turn corners can be a thing of the past.

CHAPTER XVII
EIGHT POINTED STAR

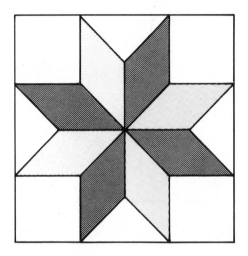

Begin as before by creating a piecing diagram, and templates. Keep grainline consistent, mark precisely, and cut leaving ample seam allowances.

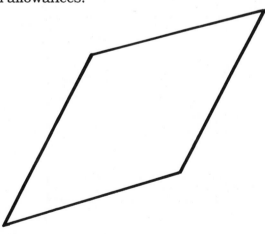

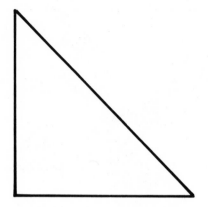

Try to avoid the urge to panic. The eight pointed star and all its beautiful variations has probably turned more would-be quilters to needlepoint than almost any other pattern. Those that stick it out are usually faced with two of life's major irritations: the hole in the middle, and the dented (or bulging) block, sometimes referred to as the "partial brassiere." Ever optimistic, many are heard to mumble these famous words, "It'll quilt out." Invisible Applique will help. Honest.

It is best to assemble the star first. Once the star is completed, applique the triangles and squares making up the rest of the block to it.

The star can be assembled in one of two ways. The first method is to sew each diamond to the one next to it, working around in a circle. The second method is to sew the diamonds in pairs first, and then sew each quarter star together to create two half stars. Then the half stars are sewn together to complete the shape. This last method offers the advantage of being able to see completed seams while sewing the last seam, giving you several points of reference.

In either case it is essential that the diamond shapes are accurately marked. The better the marking job, the easier the patches will fit together. That, and the fact that Invisible Applique allows you to work from the right side of the fabric, will help correct the aforementioned problems.

Pressing all seams in the star clockwise, or counter-clockwise, sometimes called "fanning," is helpful too, provided that none of them have been accidentally caught by your needle during the applique process. If you have a tendency to nick the seam allowance with your needle, you may want to construct the star using the first method mentioned, and fan the seams as you sew them.

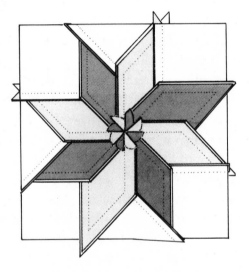

Fanning the seam allowances.

When working with stars and other blocks which require several patches to meet in the middle, worry more about matching points than pressing seam allowances under the darker patch. Fanning the seam allowances around the block is totally acceptable, since the seams are treated in a consistent manner.

CHAPTER XVIII
DRUNKARD'S PATH &
OTHER CURVED SEAMS

Prepare piecing diagram, templates, and fabric as usual, then sit back because you're in for a treat.

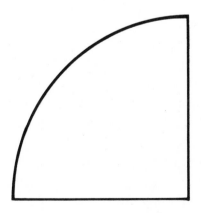

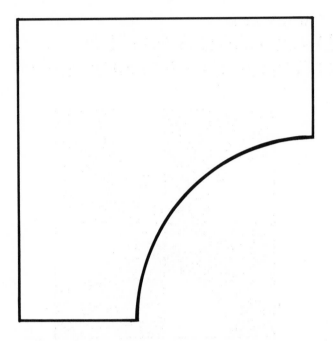

Only one assembly option makes sense when sewing a Drunkard's Path. Take advantage of the outside curve and applique the rounded wedge on to the rest of the square. There will be no clipping of curves, and you'll get to take advantage of always working on an outside curve. Joining the blocks together is as straightforward as assembling a Nine-Patch. If, when joining one unit to another, you tuck the seam allowance under the darker unit, you will be able to notch the middle join when all four units are sewn together.

The same strategy of appliqueing the outside curve on to the rest of the block will work for most any curved seam block, from Orange Peel, to Robbing Peter To Pay Paul, and from Spools, to Double Wedding Ring. Because you are appliqueing, and working from the right side of the fabric, the curved seam will pose little problem.

And, since most curved seams in patchwork are very gently curved, you can sew it quite easily the other way around, too. As a friend from Ohio once put it, "Whatever blows your skirt!"

EPILOGUE

There you have it. Invisible Applique. I haven't gotten so excited about quilting since I gave up my embroidery needle for a between and started quilting with a thimble! And, if you've stuck with me this long, I hope you've caught my enthusiasm. Invisible Applique and the quilting stitch, and you're all set. There isn't anything that you won't be able to tackle.

APPENDIX
ILLUSTRATIONS FOR LEFT-HANDED QUILTERS

Page numbers at the end of captions in the text above refer to the page in this appendix which contains a corresponding illustration redrawn for left-handed quilters. Similarly, the page numbers at the end of each caption below, refer to the page in the text showing the right-handed version of the illustration.

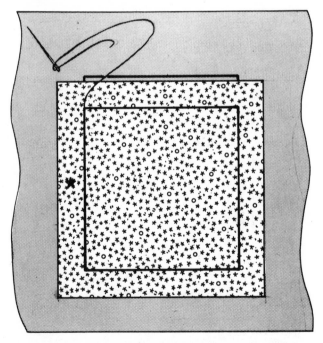

The needle exits the RIGHT side of the piece to be appliqued, in the upper left hand corner. (p. 13)

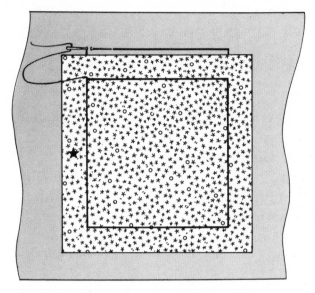

Take one small stitch in the BACKGROUND. (p. 14)

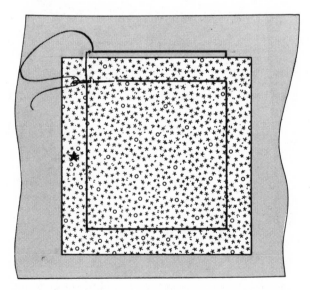

And another in the PIECE TO BE APPLIQUED. (p. 14)

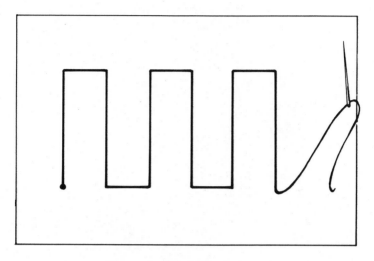

The path of the thread. (p. 15)

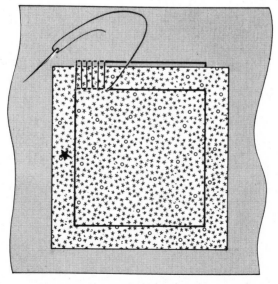

Six parallel threads are showing. (p. 16)

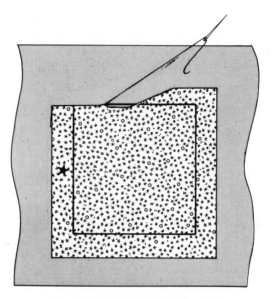

The thread disappears! (p. 17)

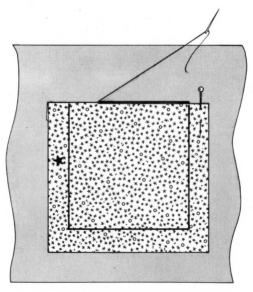

Pin in the seam allowance. (p. 18)

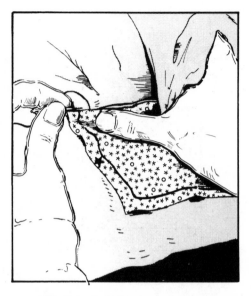

The thumb helps to expose the
background sewing line. (p. 19)

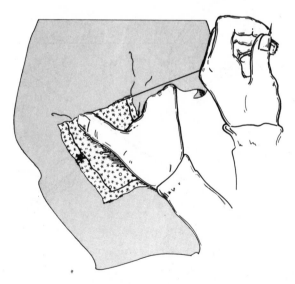

Cross the left hand over and pull. (p. 20)

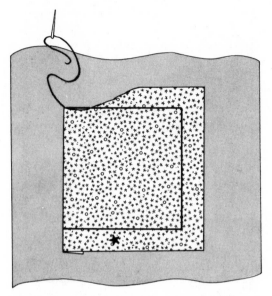

Turn under the next side and continue sewing. (p. 22)

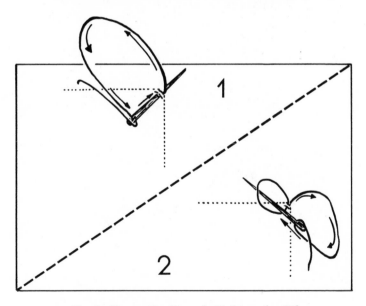

Knot off near the line of stitching. (p. 23)

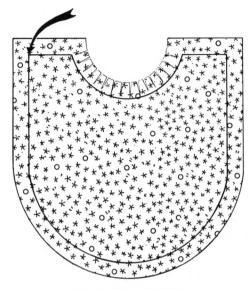

Begin here. (p. 27)

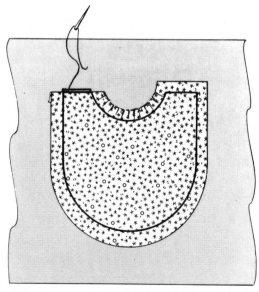

Roll under the seam allowance and begin sewing. (p. 28)

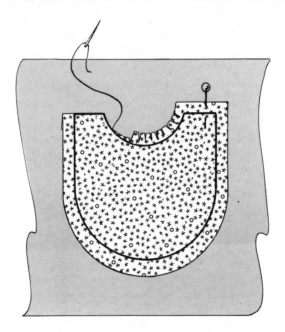

Turn under the seam allowance 1/4 inch at a time. (p. 29)

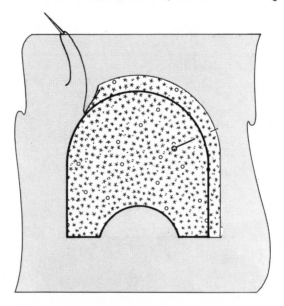

Sewing the outside curve. (p. 30)

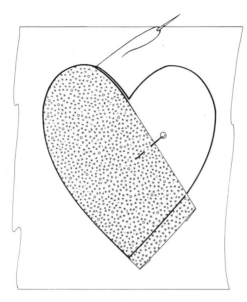

The V-shape thinks it's a straight line. (p. 33)

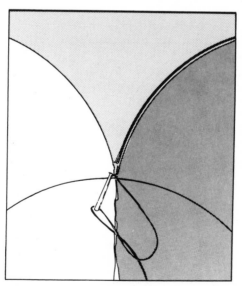

The first stitch enters the previously sewn clamshell,
and exits in the clamshell above it. (p. 49)

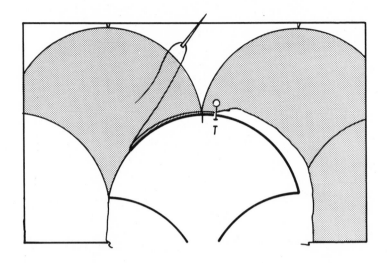

Match the Orientation Line and pin. (p. 50)

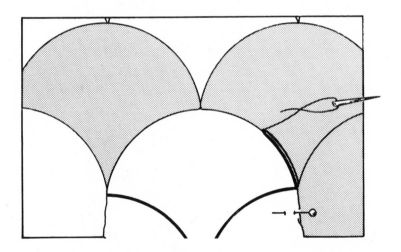

Match the end of the curve and pin. (p. 50)

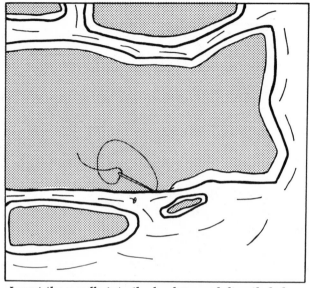

Insert the needle into the background directly below
the sewing line of the piece to be appliqued. (p. 59)

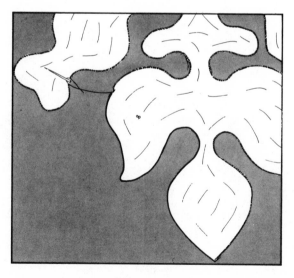

Place needle in the fold, and then directly below it. (p. 69)

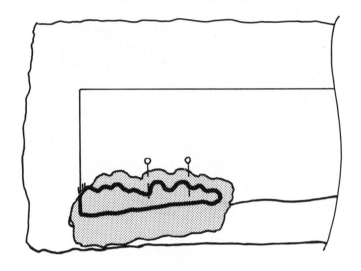

Sew the trees to the sky. (p. 89)

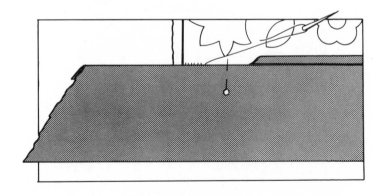

Applique the borders to the quilt top. Press. (p. 96)

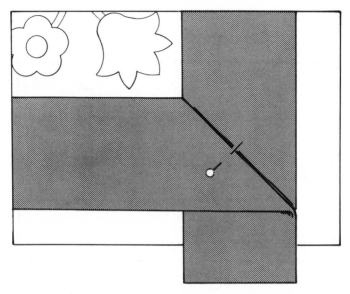

Fold one border over the other. Pin in place. (p. 96)

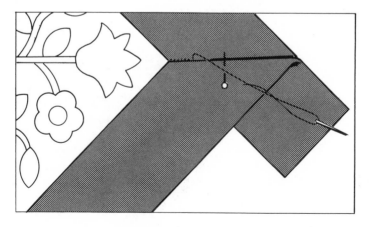

Applique as usual. (p. 97)

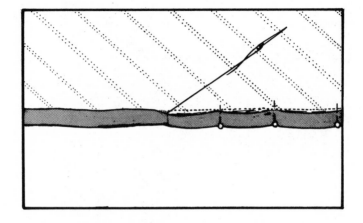

Applique the binding to the quilt. (p. 98)

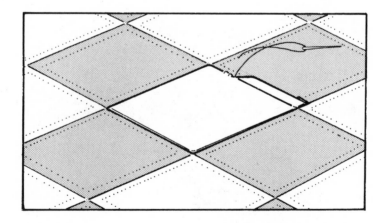

A new patch is appliqued over the old. (p. 99)

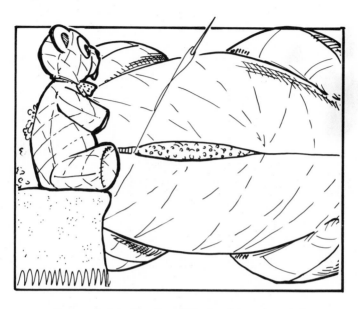

Bear repair using Invisible Applique. (p. 101)

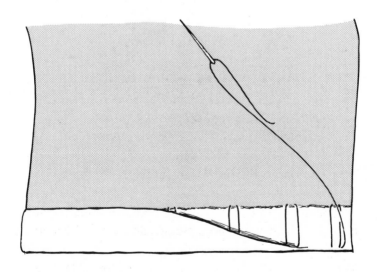

Making a rolled hem. (p. 102)

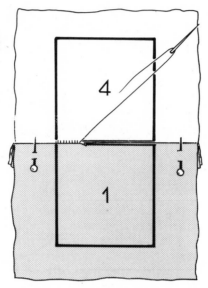

Begin to applique as usual. (p. 112)

Also by Ami Simms

How To Improve Your Quilting Stitch
Every Trick In The Book
Creating Scrapbook Quilts
How Not To Make A Prize-Winning Quilt
and
Photos-To-Fabric™ transfer paper for quilters

If you are unable to find Ami's books or transfer paper
at your favorite quilt shop, please ask for a free brochure:

Mallery Press • 4206 Sheraton Dr. • Flint, MI 48532
1-800-A-STITCH or 1-800-278-4824 or (810) 733-8743
Fax: (810) 733-7357   E-mail: amisimms@aol.com